Charmed By DARKNESS

Roger J. Morneau

Cover design by Steve Lanto
Cover design resources from iStockphoto
Inside design by Kristin Hansen-Mellish

Copyright © 2015 by Pacific Press® Publishing Association
Printed in the United States of America
All Rights Reserved

The author's estate assumes full responsibility for the accuracy of all facts and quotations as cited in this book.

Scripture quotations are from the King James Version.

You can obtain additional copies of this book by calling toll-free 1-800-765-6955 or by visiting http://www.adventistbookcenter.com.

ISBN 978-0-8163-5769-7

July 2021

Dedication

This book is dedicated in loving memory of Cynthia Grossé (1926–2014), who I looked up to as a mother figure. She was a warrior who risked her life to save my dad for God's kingdom. He would have never met and married my precious mom, Hilda, had it not been for Cynthia and Cyril.

Linda Morneau-Hatley

Contents

Foreword

ROGER J. MORNEAU (1925–1998) wrote six books that were translated into at least five languages and sold nearly a million copies. Many people remember his books about the power of prayer and his intercessory prayer ministry. But these popular books would never have been written had it not been for the people who challenged him to write his first book, *A Trip Into the Supernatural* (1982).

Many years after his conversion to Christianity, Cyril and Cynthia Grossé, the very people who studied the Bible with him in 1946, suggested that Roger should write a book about his amazing deliverance from demon worship. At first, Roger was hesitant because he was French Canadian by birth and didn't feel confident with his English writing skills. Cyril and Cynthia were successful teachers at the time and offered to type the manuscript from Roger's handwritten pages. The project took over a year to complete, and the typed manuscript was sent to the publisher. But, to their dismay, only half of the manuscript was published in *A Trip Into the Supernatural.*

During the course of working with the Morneau Estate to develop and produce a film about Roger's conversion story, we studied the full, unpublished manuscript to learn everything we could about Roger's childhood, his World War II experiences, and other factors that led him into spirit worship. The backstory included fascinating details about how God protected him even before choosing a new Master, Jesus Christ. We were equally inspired by the powerful ways the Holy Spirit taught him to pray after becoming a Christian. These unknown stories persuaded us that, by God's grace, the world should finally see the whole book, as it reveals a bigger picture of our awesome Lord.

It's been a great privilege to work with the Morneau Estate and the publisher to bring you this new book release along with never-before seen pictures and documents. And, we are grateful for Cyril Grossé and his wife, Cynthia (who passed away suddenly on December 31, 2014), and for their courageous ministry to Roger while dealing with demonic harassment. The letters, documents, pictures, and recordings they preserved all these years have been invaluable.

We believe Roger's conversion story is more relevant today than any other generation in history. The allure of spiritualism has never been stronger, and only God can deliver us from Satan's last-day deceptions. It is our sincere prayer that your eyes will be opened to the real battle being fought over every human soul and that you will trust in your Creator more than ever before. And someday soon, I look forward to meeting Roger when our Savior, Jesus Christ, calls him from the grave along with everyone else who was delivered from the charms of darkness.

Chris Lang
President
Lifestreams Media

For more information about the feature film and documentary based on this book, visit www.CharmedbyDarkness.com.

Chapter 1

A Decision for Christ

After conversing with the Lord Jesus in prayer over my problems and disposing of my three cartons of cigarettes, I sat in my rocker and picked up a book to read. As I did, the piece of paper with the message on it to phone Roland began to levitate and float around the room, then it was slapped on my open book with such force that it knocked the book out of my hands and almost off my lap. My first impulse was to tell the spirit a thing or two, but I had determined that regardless what would take place in their activities, I would not get involved in verbal communication with them. I took the piece of paper and placed it between the pages of the book and continued to read. A short while later, the book was pulled out of my hands and thrown against the wall on the opposite side of the room.

Not because of the pressure applied by the spirit, but due to respect for my friend, I decided to go and phone him. There was a pay phone in the hallway, but in this case, I would not use it, so I went to a restaurant down the street. As I sat in the phone booth, I looked at my watch; it was 1:00 A.M. The phone rang twice.

"Hello! Morneau, is this you?"

"Yes, it is."

"Morneau, you daredevil! What am I saying; I didn't mean it that way. I meant to say that you are gambling with your life; have you lost your mind?"

I replied, "You sound so upset, friend, what is your problem?"

"My problem, I have no problem; you are the one in great trouble and you sound as if you haven't got a care in the world. Morneau, I have always admired your daring spirit, but now you have gone too far; you have gone way too far. You have turned against yourself the power of the spirits that have benefited you, and you are going to be destroyed. I am surprised at the fact that you are still alive. I am concerned over you, man; it's because I care for your well-being that I have been sitting by this phone all evening waiting for your call. Don't you have anything to say?" my friend responded.

"Of course I have something to say, but how can I say anything when you have not given me a chance to talk?" I replied.

Without waiting even a moment, he went on talking again. He was very upset. "Morneau, you don't understand the extent of the trouble you are in. By Wednesday evening, according to the satanic priest, you were in deep trouble with the spirits. But now, it is too late, too late."

Chapter 2
A Miraculous Incident

It was the late part of an afternoon in November 1932, in eastern Canada. As youngsters, we had hurried home from school looking forward to at least one good hour of sledding before the evening meal. There was a lot of excitement in the air. We had an early snowfall that year, and the farm people from miles away were coming to have the grain that had been harvested that fall processed into feed for their animals and into flour for themselves. The old-timers were talking about a severe winter ahead, and that meant many rural roads would be closed for long periods of time.

My father owned a gristmill as well as a wool-carding mill, serving the many farming communities surrounding our village. It was a large three-story building; the source of power consisted of a huge waterwheel about twenty-four feet in height and ten feet wide. It operated many large pieces of machinery simultaneously, and at that particular time of the year, it ran day and night.

There was a steep hill leading to the mill that was ideal for snow sledding. The only concern we had was to make sure there were no teams of horses coming our way. All of us had a great time, especially when sledding on our stomachs while my pet dog ran after us and tried to pull our boots off.

After a while, we became very cold and I suggested that we go into the mill to warm up. I had started for the front entrance of the building when someone made the suggestion that we go in by the basement door, as he had seen a man come out that way and undoubtedly had left the door unlocked. We had been warned by our parents many times never to go into the basement of the mill when it was running, as it would be very dangerous to fall into the machinery. At the suggestion of that one friend, I replied, "It is too dangerous to go in that way."

By then, he had the door open and said, "Come on, you guys, don't be chicken. We are old enough not to walk into the machinery; besides, the buckwheat shell-fed, potbelly stove warms you up a lot faster than on the main floor. That's too slow of a process." I had to agree that what he said made a lot of sense, and I reluctantly followed everyone in.

For a few minutes, we were quietly standing by the huge potbelly stove, which in the middle was glowing red with heat. It wasn't long before we began to put some distance between it and ourselves, because the heat was reaching through our heavy clothing. We were laughing heartily, having a great time and imperceptibly getting dangerously close to what almost brought me to the portals of the grave. I was standing with my back to a machine strap fourteen inches in width that was connecting a wheel about nine feet in height and another about three feet in diameter; it was held in place by a 450-pound tightener, applying the necessary tension to keep the strap from slipping.

All of a sudden, someone tossed a glove at me and without thinking, I backed into a block of wood, which in turn caused me to fall onto that large machine strap that passed about eighteen inches from the floor. The next thing I knew, I was trapped between the nine-foot wheel and a ceiling beam, as there was no more than six inches of space between the two. An angel of the Lord must have come to my rescue, because a violent shock dislodged a three-inch steel shaft, causing the strap to fall off the three-foot wheel, which in turn caused the heavy tightener to fall down. The weight of the heavy strap pinned me on the large wheel that never slowed down.

Let me tell you, I discovered I had been blessed with a most wonderful set of lungs. I shouted, "Help! Help!" loud enough to almost wake up the dead. I was heard over the noise of heavy machinery throughout the entire place. In a moment of time, my older brother Edmond turned off the waterwheel, jumped through a hole in the floor they were fixing, and pulled me out of my predicament.

After the wheel was stopped, I found myself laying chest down on it with almost all my clothes worn off me—a very heavy winter jacket, a sweater, flannel shirt, and underwear. My left hand was hanging down along the side of the wheel, and the friction had worn off the skin and almost all the ligaments of my fingers. For a while the doctor thought he might have to amputate my hand. Today, when I wash my hands and see the large scar, I thank God for my mother, who patiently followed the doctor's advice in caring for that hand of mine so I still have the use of it.

It took three days to repair the damage done to the machinery. According to the millwright that worked on the repairs, the weight of the tightener on the strap should have crushed all my ribs as I entered under the wheel. He called it an act of God that I was alive. This experience was the talk of the town for a long time. I remember farmers coming from far away to have grain processed into flour and to express their interest in meeting the boy who had been miraculously saved from death.

This experience also served to reinforce my parents' conviction that God had a special purpose for my life. For the entire winter, I had to stay indoors, and my mother thought the time could be put to good use while my brothers and sisters were in school. Her principle project was to have me memorize the Catholic catechism. In the tender way of a Christian mother, she explained to me that in this life, people who express appreciation even for small favors are in turn benefited in greater ways. She felt that I owed it to God to acquaint myself with Him better by studying the teaching of our church, and in no better way could I do this than by memorizing a catechism. Again, she felt that in this way I could have a ready answer to meet the inquiries that would come to me concerning the teaching of my church throughout my life.

I cried many a time over my inability to retain what I was trying to memorize. My dad came to my aid. "Persistence and determination are needed," he said, "in order to succeed at this kind of a project, not crying." He shared a few easy rules, and that did it for me. He explained that mental attitude has a lot to do with whether or not one succeeds in such an undertaking. He suggested that if I looked upon the project as a hobby, it would prove to be a very rewarding experience.

How right my father was. Every day I am benefited by the counsel he gave me. Since 1946, I have memorized over two thousand verses of Scripture, which have been a source of inspiration to me and to others. By the time I was twelve years old, I had memorized two catechisms, which served to arouse in me questions regarding the character of God and the teachings of my church. I concluded that God was neither a God of love, nor was He interested in our well-being.

I would like to make a point perfectly clear. All Catholics in my childhood days were taught that the pope of Rome is the living representative of God on earth; that he is infallible; that the laws and ordinances of the church as established by the pope are the direct will of God.

From the time I made my first Communion to the time I lost my mother at twelve years of age, I had seen so many injustices and inconsistencies in the teachings of my church that it led me to lose faith in God. In fact, I came to hate God; and the day they lowered my mother in her grave, I told God I had had it with His double standards and tyrannical ways of dealing with humans. At the same time, I didn't want to break my father's heart by expressing my feelings openly, because he had more than his share of sorrows.

I had great respect for my dad and continued being obedient. I went to church every Sunday with the other members of our family, went through all the rituals, ceremonies, and so on, but from the depths of my soul, I told God that I considered Him no more noble in character than the ancient emperors of Rome, Nero and Diocletian, who had destroyed helpless people. In fact, I felt that they did not torture people in fire forever and ever, or in other words, for eternity.

Our heavenly Father's heart of love must have been saddened in seeing that the fallen cherubim with his fallen angels had succeeded in misrepresenting, under the name of religion, His just and righteous character to the point that a young boy was turning against his very Life-Giver.

Chapter 3
My Childhood Days

I was born on April 18, 1925, in Saint-Jacques, New Brunswick; a small village located about twenty miles from the border of the province of Quebec, in eastern Canada. I am the fifth child in a family of eight. My parents were very devout French Catholics. On my father's side of the family, two of his sisters were nuns, and his younger brother a priest, who became in the later years of his ministry a monsignor of the Roman Catholic Church.

Even to this day, I can't help but admire the diligence wherewith my parents followed the teachings and requirements of their church. Sincerity of heart, coupled with a great desire to please God, led them to follow the instructions of their spiritual leaders to the minutest detail.

As far back as I can remember, family prayer was a daily practice in our home. The evening prayer period I remember the best, because my knees hurt me so. The rosary was the main part of the service, and in addition to that, the repeating of the litanies of the saints was most impressive to my young mind. It consisted in calling out the names of about one hundred or more saints, and asking them to pray for us. For us children, our knees became very sore from kneeling for so long a time; we were encouraged to offer the suffering to God, so in turn He could relieve some poor soul for a short while from the torment of the flames of purgatory.

Many types of bodily humiliations were practiced in order to gain favor before God. Every Friday was a day of self-denial as pertaining to food. On the first Friday of every month, if a person went to confession and received Communion, they were assured of indulgences amounting to five thousand fewer days in purgatory for a particular soul. In those days, it meant taking no food or water from the evening before till after one had received Communion the following morning (the church has since changed this rule).

It was customary at certain times of the year for the members of our family to hold an all-night vigil. This consisted of each member kneeling for one hour before a statue and saying the rosary or other prayers. The Lent period preceding Easter was also a time of great self-mortification. My parents were God-loving people, and all activities of their lives revolved around Him. To please God was their main focus.

I remember my mother telling me many times that when I was three years old, I became very sick and the doctors gave up on my getting well. I was so ill that my dad made arrangements for my funeral. Prayers were made for my recovery, and Mother promised God that if I became well again, she would do everything in her power to see that when I grew up I would be a priest living to glorify His name and bring others to serve Him. According to her, an immediate change for the better took place, and my recovery was rapid and complete.

The time came for me to prepare for my first Communion. The more I memorized of the catechism, the commandments of the church, and so on, the more difficult I found it to harmonize the teachings of the church with the gospel of Christ.

For instance, the priest read a chapter from either one of the four Gospels or the Epistles before his sermon on Sunday, and I always enjoyed it tremendously. I remember once when I was about seven years of age, returning home from church one beautiful winter day, the sun shining brightly, there might have been twenty horse-drawn sleighs following one another; the sound of all those bells on the sleighs didn't leave much room for conversation. Not a word was spoken by anyone. Then I broke the silence by asking my mother why Jesus was so kind to people when He walked on earth, and became so mean after He went to heaven? She said, "What makes you ask that?"

I proceeded to ask, "Why would a good God turn so mean that He would burn people in purgatory for hundreds of years over little offenses souls did to Him? He certainly doesn't practice what He taught; you and Dad practice what you teach us, why doesn't He? You teach us to forgive one another's offenses, shouldn't God forgive completely?"

As I looked into my mother's tender face, I could see that she was puzzled by my reasoning. Dad tried to resolve the problem and help my mother get over the shock of my inquiries by referring to higher authorities. "You see, son, it's like your uncle Felix [the priest] once said, 'God hates sin so much, that to help people turn away from it, He had to attach such a great penalty to it; and besides, our holy father the pope knows of other good reasons why God is making use of purgatory, and we must not question his authority.' "

Oh, how I wish my parents could have discovered as I did years later that Christ, the Lord of glory, is in reality a God of love and that He does forgive completely. His heart pains over the distress of the inhabitants of this fallen world. If it were not that He has allocated a certain period of time for the fallen Lucifer and his spirit associates to manifest their true character in their great rebellion, He would have put an end to the misery of this present world, and the redeemed with immortalized bodies would now be enjoying the glory of the earth made new.

I was taught the transubstantiation doctrine, and accepted it as any other child of my age did, believing that in the Eucharist, the bread and the wine were changed by the priest into the body and blood of Christ. But on Easter Sunday 1937, the year my mother died, I heard words that led me to think differently.

The priest read from one of the Gospels concerning the resurrection of Christ; it may have been the twenty-fourth chapter of the Gospel of Saint Luke, and what fascinated me was the fact that Jesus had a hard time convincing His disciples that He was in reality resurrected; a being with real flesh and bones, and not a spirit. A couple of interesting questions popped into my mind. Could it be that heaven is a real place, like on earth, where people with flesh and bones can live real lives and not be spirits floating on clouds? If Jesus is not a spirit, how can He be in the host? Of course, I dropped the whole matter; but as I see it today, the Spirit of God must have been arresting my attention to some particular spiritual truth.

It is probably difficult for some people to understand how a small child could lose faith in God and be led to turn against religion in the way I did. Let me take you back in time to the years of 1932 to 1937, the years of the Great Depression. As I recall, there were two classes of people in those days, the "haves" and "have-nots." This I would like you to keep in mind, and see how it related to religion, and also how this served to lead me to believe that God was not just in His dealings with humankind. I will tell of three experiences that took place in our parish during that span of time. I could relate others, but I believe this will suffice to help you see my viewpoint and the impact it had on my young mind. But first, I would like to set the stage in a few words.

As a youngster, I was deeply impressed by what I heard and saw in the lives of adults. Our home was a place where peace and joy abode. Sound principles were taught to us and ruled our conduct toward others. Our parents gave us a good example of how people should get along together; kindness and consideration for others were practiced by them, and in turn, we were expected to forgive one another's shortcomings and be kind to one another. Our parents were forever helping those who were poor and in need. In my estimation of God, I felt that He should at least be as kind and compassionate toward humans as He expected them to be toward one another.

One particular experience that brought great perplexity to my mind took place in the springtime. In those days, cars were not used during the winter months, and sometimes quite an amount of work had to be done in order to get them in running order.

My dad decided to have a mechanic who lived in Edmundston come and work on his car for a couple of days, in order to get his Model A Ford in shipshape condition. Before Dad went to get this man, he made a point very clear. "The man is a Protestant," he said, "but a very fine person, and an excellent mechanic. Now, children, listen to me, it may well be that as we recite the Angelus at noon, before having our meal, that he will not participate in our devotions, and please do not stare at him; and above all, don't ask embarrassing questions pertaining to his religion, you understand?" And as he said these words, he looked directly at me.

In unison, we all replied, "Yes, Dad." For three days the man worked on Dad's car, and I enjoyed observing him work. He spoke excellent French, and of course English.

He was all that Dad had told us and more. He seemed to enjoy my talking with him, and he was kind. For instance, I found him to be very kind to the saints. Let me explain. My dad owned and operated three farms, and of course employed quite a few men. And many times I heard my dad say, when he had decided to hire a new man, "Friend, I know you and I will get along well together. I am not hard to please, but one thing I want you to never forget, my wife and I don't allow people working for us to blaspheme God or the saints; we have children we are trying to bring up to revere God, so watch your words." Notwithstanding my dad's formal counsel, I must say that many times as men were working, they forgot themselves and called down all the saints from heaven with profanities.

This mechanic I found to be amazing. If he happened to skin his knuckles, or pinch his finger, all he said was, "Ouch! That hurts!" As pertaining to the Angelus, I found him to be more reverent than we were. When Dad said, "Let us pray," he bowed his head, closed his eyes, and folded his hands. We never closed our eyes when saying the Angelus, and rushed through it as fast as possible.

After the man left, one thing troubled me greatly for days, and I could not put it out of my mind. It was something I had memorized from the catechism, *"Hors de l'Église Catholique Apostolique et Romaine il n'y a point de salut,"* translated, "Outside of the Roman Catholic Church there is no salvation."

My mother sensed that my mind was taken up with something that was of great importance to me and said, "Is something troubling you? I have noticed you have been so quiet for the last few days."

I said, "Mother, where do the good Protestants go when they die?"

"That is a good question, son, why do you ask?" I quoted her what I had memorized from the catechism. She admitted she did not know, and that we should ask Father Morneau when he came to visit us. That inquiry of mine must have troubled my mother also, for at the evening meal that day, Mother told Dad what we had talked about, and asked his viewpoint on the subject.

Dad didn't have a sure answer to the question, but made the statement that he felt that God wouldn't leave a good person out of heaven, regardless of whether he was a Catholic or a Protestant. He enlarged upon it by saying that probably what happens when a good Protestant dies is that the angels lead him through the back door. He continued by saying, "Protestants do not have the glory of being welcomed by Saint Peter personally, but they shouldn't care as long as they get in. They shouldn't expect to be treated as celebrities; after all, their forefathers made a bad mistake when they left the Catholic Church, and all their descendants can expect to suffer on account of it." I felt that my dad's reasoning was probably correct, but again those solemn words kept coming to my mind. "Outside of the Roman Catholic Church there is no salvation."

A few months went by, and finally we heard that Uncle Felix was coming to visit all the relatives. I asked my dad if he could, when the opportunity presented itself, ask Uncle Felix about the good Protestants, and he agreed.

The day Uncle Felix visited our home I figured would be the day the question perplexing my mind would be wiped away forever. On the contrary, I received the shock of my life. After the formalities were over, and the visiting had gone on for quite a while, Dad turned to my uncle and said, "Felix, tell me, where do the good Protestants go when they die?"

In turn, my uncle said, "Why do you ask?" Dad proceeded to tell him about my inquiring, in the light of what the catechism said, that "outside of the Roman Catholic Church there is no salvation."

My uncle's reply was, "What Roger has quoted to you from the catechism is correct, there is no salvation outside of the Catholic Church, regardless of whom the person may be." This opened up quite a debate on the matter; Dad claiming it wouldn't be fair of God not to let a good Protestant into heaven. My uncle took the heat out of the conversation by making the statement that it could be that the souls of good Protestants probably go to limbo at death—the place where the souls of infants who have not been baptized go when they die. My uncle continued by saying, "One thing I know, according to the church, no Protestant, good or bad, will go to heaven or will ever see God. And remember, I didn't make the rules, I only teach them, and if there were any possible way for a Protestant to get to heaven, our holy father the pope surely would have told us."

That experience placed a big question mark in my mind concerning the justice of God. Time went by, and a couple of years later, God's justice was again scrutinized through human inquiries.

It was a beautiful July evening, and about eight thirty, someone passing by stopped to tell my parents that a neighbor had died suddenly while working about five miles from home. One statement made by the man brought consternation to all present. "He died without having a priest to give him the last sacrament of the church." He mentioned that the dead man's brother was bringing the body home.

While shaking his head from side to side, he left saying, "It's sad, sad, sad."

I can remember that incident as if it were yesterday. It wasn't long before we saw a dilapidated, horse-drawn wagon moving slowly down the road. In the back was a body covered with a blanket, and the driver sat on the front of the wagon, his legs dangling down and his countenance reflecting the despair of his soul.

Sitting with us on the front porch were a couple of neighbors who had come to use our phone as they often did—our family having one of only two telephones for miles around. After the body had passed our house, my mother commented on how sad it was, and added, "If only he could have had a priest to forgive his mortal sins, so that he would not find himself going into hellfire. Let's hope he only had venial sins on his soul; this alone represents years of burning in the flames of purgatory."

My dad picked up the conversation by saying, "We'll have to get a few dollars together and have masses celebrated for the peace of his soul, for I can't see how his widow and the kids will be able to do so."

One of the neighbors spoke up and said, "I feel like telling you to save your money. I am inclined to think that his soul is now in hellfire. You see, Mr. and Mrs. Morneau, this man is known to have had sticky fingers; what I mean to say is that he has at times taken things that were not his."

My dad was shocked for a moment or two, and after regaining his composure, said, "This is quite a revelation to me. Listen, everyone, I want you all to know that in the sight of God, I am giving to the dead man the chain he has borrowed from me, and anything that I am not aware of, I give it to him also. In this way, his soul is freed from any condemnation he may have brought upon himself in the sight of God."

The neighbor spoke again, but this time it was to compliment Dad on his character. "Mr. Morneau, I don't mean to be irreverent toward God, but right now I feel that you are kinder of character than He is. I must admit that this is the nicest gesture toward anyone I have ever seen or heard of. In fact, you may be the first human being forcing God to take a soul out of hellfire and placing him in purgatory till he is purified enough to enter heaven."

That experience made quite an impact upon my mind, something never to be forgotten. For many days that incident kept passing before my mind. As I meditated upon it, I felt as though the neighbor had said that my dad was of more noble character than the God he served. I concluded that God was most unkind in causing souls to suffer in purgatory because the relatives had no money to have masses celebrated for their loved ones who died during the hard times of the Great Depression.

One experience that served to turn me completely against God was that of my own mother passing away. I like to clarify this statement by saying that it had a double effect upon me, as I will relate in the next few pages.

It was the spring of 1937, and Mother was admitted to the hospital for an operation. After a couple of weeks, she was sent home to live out her last days. Being twelve years old, I was at a very impressionable age. For instance, I believe some of the last words my mother spoke to me before she died have led me years later to become a commandment keeper—including the fourth commandment. Or, in other words, become an observer of the seventh-day Sabbath.

Arriving home from school one day, I went into her bedroom to give her a kiss on the forehead as I did daily. Mother said to me, "Please sit down, I would like to say something that I feel is very important to both of us. As you know, I have but a short while to be with you, and I want you to remember this bit of advice. As you make your way through life, apply yourself to show appreciation to people for the kindness they show toward you. As I have said in the past, give thanks even if people give you as little as a glass of water. In this life, people who express appreciation for small favors are in turn benefited in greater ways." I promised Mother I would apply myself in carrying out her advice as she wished me to. It has become a well-established habit in my life.

After World War II was over, and having lived a godless life for many years, in a most unique way, God allowed me to come into a position in life that enabled me to understand eternal realities as they truly are. I was made to comprehend the great controversy between the forces of good and evil in its reality. And above all, to understand the immeasurable love of God as manifested toward me, an undeserving human being, in the most precious of ways. A sincere desire then swelled up in my heart to show appreciation to the Creator. At that time, I became acquainted with words spoken by our Lord on that subject: "If ye love me, keep my commandments" (John 14:15). This I decided to do, and have done since 1946. It may not be popular among the Christian churches of the day, but it brings contentment to my heart in knowing that doing so is pleasing to God. Now back to 1937.

In those days, it was customary for the dead to be viewed in their homes instead of at a funeral parlor. For three days, friends, relatives, and neighbors came to pay their respects and pray for my mother's soul. On the day of the funeral, most people present felt that our mother was in heaven next to God because of the many rosaries recited for her. But that which made us feel best was the fact that Dad had arranged to have Gregorian masses offered for the peace of her soul.

As our uncle Felix explained to us, Gregorian masses are the most wonderful thing that can happen to someone's departed soul. He explained how this had been devised by Pope Gregory, who had a special concern for souls in purgatory. An arrangement is made to have three hundred masses celebrated at the exact same time on a particular day; it takes place in various parishes, convents, monasteries, and so on. According to what he told us, this mass arrangement has a redeeming power sufficient to take a soul directly to heaven so that it will not even see the flames of purgatory.

On that same day, I heard one of the relatives make the statement that Gregorian masses cost one dollar each or, in other words, three hundred dollars for the entire arrangement. The thought entered my mind that we were very fortunate that our father could afford to help our mother get to heaven so nicely. Then I thought of a woman who had died six months earlier in our parish. The family was too poor to have any masses celebrated; she would have to suffer in purgatory. My mind was carried back to the day she had died. Her funeral arrangements had upset my dad greatly, as he was a member of the welfare committee of our parish.

I recall Dad coming home that evening. He sat down for his evening meal and then decided he would pass it up. My mother, realizing that something was bothering him, asked if something was wrong. Dad's reply was, "Yes, I might as well tell you. I have spent the better part of the afternoon at the church presbytery with other members of the welfare committee discussing the problems concerning the poor in our parish. The main item of concern was the purchasing of a coffin for old Annie. I wasn't against trying to save a little money, but when Father Paquin asked the funeral director how much we would save if the crucifix and handles of the coffin were removed before burial, I became very upset and felt like giving the good father a piece of my mind, but I held back because of due respect for his high office. To put an end to the discussion, I said I would pay the difference in the cost. It's a sad, sad thing to be poor in this day and age, especially when it comes to dying."

As I thought about both incidents, I couldn't help but feel that God was most unjust by allowing the misery going on in this world to continue. As time went on, I lost confidence in God and the church and determined to have nothing to do with either, as soon as I would be old enough to be on my own. In the fall of 1937, my brother Edgar and I were sent to a boarding academy operated by the nuns of *L'Hotel Dieu de Saint-Basile.* I received a great deal more religious instructions, which only served to further harden my heart. From outward appearances, no one would have dreamed of the conflict going on in my soul. A few years went by, then World War II came along, and with it a call to serve one's country.

Chapter 4
The War Years

I felt attracted to the Canadian Merchant Navy, because someone I knew had joined and told me how much he enjoyed it. It gave you a secure feeling to have the Royal Canadian Navy and Air Force watching over you, seeing that merchant shipping was looked upon as the lifeline of the armed forces.

For two and a half years, I worked in the engine room operation of the ships I sailed on—most of the time as a fireman. I can remember coming on watch and saying to myself, "I hope no torpedo comes sailing into these boilers while I stand here." Today, I thank God that none did; for a number of men that I knew were not as fortunate. That merchant navy experience served to harden me more and cause me to lose faith in God and man.

During 1942 and 1943, supreme effort was being put forth on the part of Nazi Germany's navy to sink all shipping out of Canada destined for war zones. The fighting in the North Atlantic was the fiercest at this time, and German U-boats were concentrating their efforts in a pattern that became known as the wolf-pack approach to sea combat.

For a while, we became involved in carrying cargo from Montreal and Quebec City to the coast of Labrador (Goose Bay) and a place called Sept-Îles on the north shore of the Gulf of Saint Lawrence for the building of air bases jointly constructed by the governments of Canada and the United States.

U-boat crews were determined to do away with not only the Allies' precious cargos, but with those who manned the ships also. It seemed that their favorite time to attack was just at the break of day. Many times as ships were torpedoed and the crew made their escape in life boats, a sub would surface and then machine-gun everyone. Some convoys were sunk in their entirety.

It was a rule at the time that every one of our crew spent at least two hours per day on deck watch, even if one was working in the engine room. My deck time fell between 2:00 and 4:00 A.M., and at that time of night, combat action was not so likely due to darkness. I recall the one night I came on watch without having had to make use of my alarm clock to get me up.

About 1:00 A.M., coming out of a deep sleep, I sat right up in bed. It was dead silent; the engines had come to a standstill. That familiar humming of engines telling propellers to churn more and more water in obedience to the wish of man had stopped. It was pitch black that night; in fact, so much so that I thought someone had closed the portholes in my cabin (as part of war regulations, all glass portholes had been painted black for the duration). I jumped out of my bunk and checked them to make sure they were really closed, before turning on the light to get dressed. To my amazement, they were wide open.

In a few minutes, I was out on deck talking to one of the watchmen concerning our lack of action—travel action, that is. He stated that our wireless operator had received word from one of the Royal Navy torpedo boats that submarine activity had been detected in close proximity and a command to shut off our engines was given.

I went on watch a little earlier that night in order to give the fellow I was relieving a chance to get himself some well-deserved rest. About three o'clock, the first mate, being unable to sleep and having walked the decks over many times, came to me and said, "Morneau, I am very restless tonight; I have the impression that something awful is going to happen, and somehow I feel kind of relaxed every time I chat with you on my walks about the ship. So I am going to sit here in this canvas chair and try to get some rest. I have the impression that God has special care over you. I don't know why, but I do."

As we were conversing, the mate said, "I have seldom seen the sea so calm; I wish it would build up a storm for our safety."

I replied to his statement as I kept gazing into the dark, trying to locate what I hoped would never appear—the outline of an enemy submarine. After a couple of minutes had passed in silence, I said, "Mate, tell me some of your hero stories." There was no answer. I turned around and said, "Mate, are you OK?" His reply came in the form of a deep relaxed snore, followed by more of the same; he was sound asleep.

Then the words he had said about finding a relaxing atmosphere at my side, and his feeling of God having special care over me, fastened themselves on my mind, even though I refused to believe them; and they repeated themselves afresh many times in the months to follow. Yes, something terrible did happen that night; ships were torpedoed at daybreak, but we escaped untouched.

Charmed by Darkness

Once we left the port of Quebec City, and after two hours of sailing, the captain came on deck, opened a large envelope, and read our sailing orders. Because the two convoys had been sunk but a few days apart at the entrance of the Gulf of Saint Lawrence, we were shortly to be joined by torpedo boats of the Royal Navy, and with air coverage from the Canadian Air Force, we were to proceed to the Atlantic, where some of the ships were to change course depending on their destination. Ours was Newfoundland.

Out of the thirteen ships, ours was the only one to proceed past Anticosti Island. As we entered the harbor of Corner Brook, Newfoundland, we found everyone greatly surprised to see us. A report had reached them that our convoy had been sunk. Today, I agree with the old sea wolf that God took special care of me while I was surrounded by danger of all types. By the power of His love, He overruled in the affairs of men and preserved my life from the hand of the destroyer.

A quick, unexpected turn of events took me away from sailing for seven months, and almost brought me to perish in Europe during a major Allied offensive. It was customary as we were docked at port for someone from the harbor master's office to bring mail aboard. On this occasion, I had a dispatch from the Royal Canadian Mounted Police (RCMP) to report immediately to them on arrival, as my army draft exemption had not been renewed in Ottawa by the merchant navy's headquarters for the following six months. I was shocked by the news and proceeded to look into it. I made an unexpected visit to the Montreal office of the merchant navy and asked to see Mr. McMaster, the shipping director, who had signed me in two and a half years before. The young receptionist asked if I had an appointment to see him, and my reply was, "I do not, and I will turn this place upside down, if I don't get to see him."

She replied, "Seeing that you insist, I'll try to comply." She soon returned with the gentleman following her.

"Hi! Frenchie," said Mr. McMaster. "What can I do for you? Please come into my office so we can talk."

I handed him the dispatch from the RCMP with the command, "You explain this to me." He immediately called in his secretary, and asked her to check with the person responsible to see that the names of all seamen be processed with the defense department in Ottawa twice a year as demanded by the federal government, to assure themselves that every able-bodied person was part of the war effort.

It wasn't long before the disturbing news was brought to him that somehow the name of Roger J. Morneau had been left off the list of all those hundreds of names of seamen in active service sent to the defense department just a month before. Mr. McMaster could hardly believe it. Nothing like this had taken place before. He went on to assure me that all would be well after he completed a long-distance telephone call to an army colonel with whom he often transacted a great many defense matters.

The part of the phone conversation that I heard went like this: "Good day, Colonel, how are you today? Say, I have a problem that I feel you alone can solve at this late hour." He went on telling him of my predicament, and my having to report to the RCMP with the possibility of being drafted into the army. He continued by saying, "Colonel, I hope you can reverse this action for us. You can't! What do you mean your hands are tied? You can't be serious. I am fast losing confidence in your word, sir. How can you expect me to feel differently, when I see that the understanding we have established between our departments at the outbreak of the war doesn't seem to matter too much anymore. Let me assure you, Colonel, that I am going to get my way when it comes to keeping this man from going into your army. If you can't help me, I'll find someone who will, even if it means my working day and night on this problem, and I will not stop if need be till I reach the prime minister of Canada, goodbye."

After ending his phone conversation, Mr. McMaster seemed dazed, and he kept saying, "I can't believe it, I can't believe it. This military officer couldn't be less interested in trying to help us solve this difficulty." As I looked at the man, his facial expressions were such that I thought he might be working himself into a heart attack. My anger abated, and I began to feel sorry for him as I saw that he was genuinely sincere in trying to reverse the tide of events and keep me in the merchant navy.

I tried to soften the blow he had unexpectedly received by saying, "Mr. McMaster, you are taking this thing too much to heart. Let's forget the whole matter. As for me, I am going directly to the army recruiting center after leaving here, and will enlist in active service immediately. If I may use your own words, sir, I can't see myself sitting back waiting for a final decision from the Canadian Army, while you struggle through the dilemma that I can imagine you would have to go through in trying to retrieve me from their powers."

He then sat back in his desk chair somewhat resigned and said, "Roger, regardless of whether or not you join the army at this time, let me tell you that I am not going to give up on this project of getting the Canadian Army to honor their word, even if it is the last thing I do in my living days. Our legal department will start to work on this case today, and I can assure you that along the way some of those high-ranking army officers are going to eat humble pie before this matter is over with."

I wished the man good luck in this undertaking, even though I felt he was wasting his efforts, and left his office. After enlisting in the army, I was for some time stationed in Kingston, Ontario, and then went to Camp Borden in the same province for training. The experience was interesting and somewhat challenging, and I enjoyed it.

Again I found myself going to church. But this time it was forced upon me. In those days, every soldier had to go to church, whether he wanted to or not.

One either joined the Catholic or Protestant church parade; we were given that choice. I told my sergeant I would join the Protestant church parade. He asked why, and made mention of the fact that I might create bad feelings between the Catholic and Protestant boys in our platoon, seeing that it had happened in the past under similar circumstances. I assured the sergeant that I was not a troublemaker. I would go to church with the Protestants to find out exactly what they protest about.

So I went to the church of my choice, and after a few months, I concluded that the only differences existing from the Catholics was that every Protestant soldier had a Bible in the pew to read from, there was no praying to the saints, and no talk of purgatory. Concerning God, the Protestant chaplains made Him such a God of love that everyone would get into heaven as long as they believe that He exists. For those who did not believe in God, they would have to pay for their unbelief by spending eternity in a lake of fire, and that would serve them right.

I must say that I did hear one of the best hellfire sermons I had ever heard. Talk about scaring people into heaven, that preacher really knew how. All of the fellows seemed to agree that this was the time to get on the good side of God. As for me, I didn't hesitate to tell my buddies that I felt that if God was as loving as He had been said to be the previous Sundays, He wouldn't be the type to carry on a never-ending punishment on helpless human beings. And on the other hand, if He were heartless enough to carry on a never-ending punishment, I wouldn't want to have Him for my God. I was surprised to hear some of the fellows say that my reasoning was logical from a human viewpoint, and that maybe they were being instructed incorrectly.

Time has a way of changing days into weeks, and weeks into months. So it was that we became accustomed to military life, while our company was in specialized training. The day came when the countdown for the last month of our training began. Many of the soldiers had a calendar upon which they crossed out the date at the end of each day. Some of the servicemen objected to their comrades following that procedure, claiming that it only served to spell out "combat duty soon to come."

Tension was mounting on every side. The war theater of Europe was producing a superabundance of bad news. On the other hand, the holiday season was approaching, and with it a thirty-day furlough that was supposed to take place after our training and before shipping overseas. Unknown to any of us at that time was that the urgency of the hour was soon to consume that well-deserved furlough, robbing almost all the men of the precious privilege of seeing their loved ones for the last time. A few months later, almost the entire company was wiped out in Europe.

As for me, an event that began as a bitter experience turned out to be a savor of life unto life. It was early December, our training being completed, life had slowed down to an unusual pace. For about a week, except for some morning assignments, the remainder of the day was ours to use as we saw fit. However, no passes were given out to anyone desiring to leave camp. Then came a big surprise that materialized in the middle of the night.

I recall that on this particular day boredom had set in, and a sense of frustration was being experienced by a great many of the men. By midevening, I noticed that the usual mood of the fellows in our barracks had changed. Most of them were not talkative, card playing was down to a minimum, and letter writing had come to a halt. Many with pen in hand and only a few words on paper could not proceed any further and were telling of their predicament to others. It had been impossible for them to find out from their commanding officers if and when they would be going on furlough. The main questions heard were, "What should I say to my parents, or wife, or girlfriend, regarding the furlough we are supposed to get?"

The evening went by, and when the time came to retire for the night, someone made the statement that the day should be remembered as "the day when all military pens came to a standstill in Company 21." The lights were turned off in the barracks, and there was silence.

The next thing I knew, at 3:00 A.M., the lights went on, the bugle sounded, and our sergeant shouted, "Everyone at attention!"

All of us were shocked out of dreamland into reality. We jumped out of our beds and stood at attention. The sergeant proceeded to inform us of what was taking place. "Fellows, our company has received its marching orders, and we will be leaving Camp Borden on short order. All of you need to appear in the parade hall fully dressed in forty-five minutes to receive detailed information on the matter. You are dismissed."

As we entered the parade hall, we found that there were twenty-one hundred men making up ten companies, with the same bewildered look on their faces. It wasn't long before we were commanded to fall into ranks. One of the top brass came up to a lectern, adjusted the mic to the correct height, then informed us in this way:

"We have received from the Department of War in Ottawa the following order: All furloughs and leaves of all types have been canceled. This applies to all men present here, except one individual whose name I will give in a few minutes. This entire battalion is moving on to Halifax, Nova Scotia, and from there to Europe."

He paused for a few moments while a wave of whispers on the part of the twenty-one hundred men built up to a crescendo that peaked into a sound similar to that of a waterfall. All around me I heard men saying, "I can't believe this!" "That's not fair!" "How am I going to tell my parents about this?" and so on.

He continued by saying, "I personally feel sorry that you men will not be with your families for the holiday season as you had planned, seeing that you were promised and are entitled to have a thirty-day furlough that was to start the day after tomorrow. But, men, we can't let this disappointment dishearten us; we are living in a time of great national emergency, and I know that you agree with me, that unless we sacrifice ourselves for the well-being of our nation, our loved ones may in the near future lose the freedoms that we all have enjoyed to this day. Now, I must say, that all men will have to be fully packed, having had one's breakfast, and standing by the platform of the train depot to ship out at seven A.M. today."

He then placed down on the lectern the document he had held in his hand and picked up another one. Again, he spoke in these words: "I have here an order regarding the one individual who will not be shipping out. Private Roger Morneau, will you raise your right hand?"

I couldn't believe my ears, in fact, I thought I had not heard correctly, and didn't react immediately. So he repeated what he had said, and as he did so, my sergeant turned to me and said, "That's you, man." My hand shot right up.

The colonel continued, "Private Morneau, you will not be going along, so report to your commanding officer for further instruction on this matter as soon as this gathering is dismissed." He turned to the captain and said, "Captain, carry on."

The captain came up to the mic and shouted, "Companies, fall out!"

Immediately, the sound of a great commotion was heard throughout the building as those hundreds of men began to mill around and talk about the unexpected occurrence. The fellows in my platoon began to tell me how lucky I was. But my reaction of the news was the complete opposite of what most everyone would have expected it to be. The thought that immediately entered my mind was that I would probably be in camp a month or two, then find myself shipped to Europe with an entirely new group of men. I was getting along nicely with everyone in my platoon and didn't want to be separated from them. I turned to my sergeant and said, "Please try to help me stay with this company."

His reply was, "I'll do my best, but first let's find out the reason for the order."

He went to pick up the order and came back with a piece of paper that said just about nothing. It read something like this: "To the Army Command of Camp Borden: concerning the departure of the army battalion from Camp Borden for Nova Scotia, as per Order Number ___, from the Canadian Department of the Army, the only exception to the marching order is here explained: Be herewith instructed that without fail Private Roger J. Morneau is to be retained in Camp Borden till additional correspondence reaches you on the matter, which will be in the near future. He will not be made to rejoin the battalion at a later date. All correspondence on this matter should indicate Confidential File Number ___. Sincerely, ___________."

By then our company lieutenant had come to see what it was all about. He read the message, rubbed his chin, and said, "This is most unusual." He continued by saying, "Let me suggest to you that your sergeant take you through the chain of command until you get someone with enough authority to find out for you what this is all about. I don't want you to live in suspense for days, maybe even weeks." He then turned to the sergeant, saying, "I'd like you to take this man to Captain __________ immediately."

In a short while, the captain was reading the mysterious memorandum from Ottawa. He began asking me questions that could lead me to think of something that could relate to the inexplicable piece of paper, but to no avail. The next step was to take me to the major. The captain picked up the phone and called the major's quarters to find out when the officer would be getting up, and at what time I could stand before him, as it was urgent. He was told that the high brass had gone to bed at midnight, and had left an order to call his residence at 4:30 A.M., as he wanted to get up early because of the activities taking place in the camp. A call back was promised to take place shortly, and so it did; the phone rang, and the message came that the major would see us at 5:30 A.M., or in other words, in a half hour.

The sergeant and I jumped into a jeep and rushed as fast as possible to keep our appointment. We entered the place and were told to sit down and that we would have to wait for a few minutes. The aide added the comment that the major wasn't too pleased by his attention being requested so early in the morning. After the aide had left us, the sergeant commented that the time of day was working against our best interest and that I should not be disappointed if I received anything but help.

A short while later, we were told we could enter the officer's office. The aide led us in, told us to sit down, and left. The major was reading something, and his desk was set so that he would have to turn his head some in order to see us. But the mood he was in did not permit him to do so. Again, the sergeant looked at me and rolled his eyes, giving me to understand that someone didn't care for our presence.

Then as the officer lifted his eyes from his reading material and turned toward us, his stern-looking countenance changed to one of genuine friendliness, with the pleasant inquiry, "Roger! What in the world brings you here at this time of day?" My sergeant's jaw fell. He couldn't believe his eyes and ears; he shook his head a little, probably to make sure he wasn't dreaming.

There I was standing before an officer for whom I had been working every Saturday throughout the summer months. I had been assigned to mow the lawn around his house on a voluntary basis, and quite frequently we had chatted together, and at times had had a cool beverage sitting on his front porch with him and his wife.

My problems were over; from then on all was very encouraging. Talk about someone being willing to help me, the man went out of his way, all out. First, he suggested that we get ourselves some breakfast and get back to his office at 7:30

A.M. He would then contact a very close friend of his, a senior attorney in the defense department in Ottawa. He would phone him at his residence, and wanted me present in his office while the call was being made.

The major held the memo in his left hand, and with the index finger of his right hand, lightly struck the piece of paper two or three times while saying, "Confidential File Number ___. Roger, your case has got to be something unique. I am impressed with the thought that somehow a legal element is attached to this. Have you applied to go into secret service work for the Dominion?"

"No, sir, I have not."

Then jokingly he said, "You are not suing the government of Canada for anything, are you?"

"No, sir, I wouldn't want to do a thing like that." Then, like a flash of lightning, the thought entered my mind that the merchant navy might be doing something of that caliber, and I spilled out the words, "Oh! Maybe, yes, it could be!"

The major was motivated out of his chair, and with a sobering countenance replacing a jovial one, said, "What is this you are saying?"

"Sir, I didn't think of it till now. Really, sir, I have no contention with any branch of our government, but right now I am under the impression that the merchant navy may have been fighting the Department of the Army in the courts." Then I went on to explain my transition from sailing to carrying a gun for the military.

"That's it, Roger. I can see where there's probably a lot of heat being applied somewhere and your presence is being requested. And things look good for you." Pointing to the memo, he said, "You will not be rejoining the battalion; that spells out good news. Man, I am getting excited over this. And remember this, whatever takes place from now on, I will be working for your interests. Now, go, go, go, so you can be back at seven thirty."

We jumped into the jeep, and my sergeant was as excited over what he had heard and what was likely to take place as would a seven-year-old tyke who had been promised to visit the monkeys at a zoo. At our return, we were ushered immediately into the presence of the major. He closed the morning paper he was reading, had us sit ourselves comfortably, picked up the phone, and dialed. The part of the conversation that I could hear went like this:

"Good morning, Mary, this is Jim. How are you today? Oh, thank you, Mary, Ann and I were conversing last evening about the wonderful time we had at your place last month. We are looking forward to having the opportunity to return the courtesy. Is Harry available? Hello, Harry. Real fine, thank you. Harry, I have a unique problem and thought of seeking your help to expedite matters. I have a young man in my office that is being held back from shipping out with a battalion leaving Camp Borden this morning. He is very distressed over the matter, and I am trying to help him out. I'd like to read you a memo, the only material we have received from the defense department."

After having read the memorandum, the officer then related for a minute or two what I had told him earlier, and listened to his attorney friend's conversation, except for the exclamations of interest here and there on what he was being told. "Harry, what you have told me is indeed interesting, and if I call you after nine you could very well have all the information we are looking for. Wonderful. I'll talk to you later."

He hung up the phone, sat back in his deluxe office chair, and smiled, indicating contentment, and said, "My friend Harry is a colonel in charge of the Department of Legal Affairs for the Canadian Army. He tells me that your case may be the one brought to his attention a while back. It had to do with a military officer having made an awful goof; an awful bad decision pertaining to a seaman versus military service, and the merchant navy took the matter through the courts and caused an awful lot of embarrassment to that particular officer and his superiors."

The major then stood up, walked behind his chair, placed both his hands on the back of the chair, giving us the impression that the next few words would be of great importance and worth listening to. "Now, Roger, I don't want to give you false hopes, so don't build up your expectations to the point that you will be unhappy if what I am going to tell you doesn't become reality. My attorney friend said that if you are the former seaman involved in that court case, you will undoubtedly be given an honorable discharge from the Canadian Army." He then sat down and picked up the memo, his behavior indicating that there was more to come.

"Maybe I shouldn't tell you this, I may find myself doing the very thing I just told you not to do—build up your hopes. But I cannot resist my inclination to tell you. Harry said that he is 90 percent sure that your name is that of a seaman getting that discharge from the army." That bit of information was beginning to reveal what shortly became for me a joyous experience of being given great respect by the military, accompanied by the type of treatment usually accorded persons of exceptional importance.

The major first told us we could go and return to his office at 9:00, then changed his mind. "Somehow, I feel impressed," he said, "that I may need you before nine. Fellows, I'll have my aide take you to our staff lounge, where you can have a hot beverage and relax while waiting." We agreed and left. It must have been about 8:45 when the aide was back to get us.

"On the double, men, the major is on the phone with Ottawa and is waiting for you."

"Roger, you lucky fellow," said the major, "we have excellent news for you. How would you like to go home on a thirty-day furlough?" Without waiting for my answer, he went right on filling me in on the details. "You are being held back due to the fact that you will be discharged from the army in January. I'll tell you more about it after I am off the phone."

Of course, my reply was highly positive. "Sir, I am delighted at the thought of going home, seeing that you have the way open for me to do so." The officer continued his phone conversation by saying, "Would you be kind enough to send me a telegram right away to back up what you have just told me? And I will send Private Morneau home on furlough today." He said Thank you and hung up the phone.

The major went on explaining that a long legal struggle between the Canadian Army and the merchant navy had just ended in Ottawa when one of the highest courts in the land gave the military an unexpected blow in a decision stating that the army had violated a constitutional law of Canada by not respecting the dedicated efforts the Canadian Merchant Navy was making toward winning the war.

The merchant navy's charter, as set forth by the federal government of Canada, had been violated by the army in their dictatorial course of action taken toward a sailor in good standing, when they set forth in turning over to the Royal Canadian Mounted Police the name of that particular individual as if he was violating a law of the land, without first consulting with the shipping director on what had happened when they found his name missing on the biyearly report.

The major was very happy for me. He shook my hand and congratulated me and the merchant navy for giving some of the army brass "a kick in the backside, it being just what they deserved" (using the major's own words).

The officer was radiant with enthusiasm over my good fortune, and manifested it in some quick action. He proceeded in finding out what the train's schedule was, leaving Camp Borden for Toronto on that day. The timetable indicated a departure at 11:00 A.M. and another toward the evening.

The major turned to his aide and said, "Have someone start working immediately on getting a round-trip railway ticket for Private Morneau, from Camp Borden to Edmundston, New Brunswick. Have someone else process a furlough pass." He then picked up the phone and asked his private secretary to come into his office as he wished to dictate a letter.

While doing that, the aide was leaving to execute his command, but the major gave him the stop signal by putting up his right hand. The receiver was replaced on the phone, and he proceeded to give his aide one last task to do. "I want you to phone the paymaster as soon as possible, and instruct him to figure up the sum Private Morneau is entitled to receive having completed basic training, plus six months of specialized training, and for him to have a check ready to pick up in one hour."

Action, yes there was action; everyone was on the double. The office door opened, and as the aide proceeded out, the stenographer walked in.

"Good morning, Diane," said the major.

"Good morning to you also, sir," replied the young lady.

"Diane, I want you to type a letter on my personal stationery, which I will sign when completed, and please make it as impressive as possible both in appearance and content. I am trying to impart dignity and honor, the sum of which is highly deserved by the person who will be carrying that letter."

I could hardly believe my ears that the words just spoken by the major were intended for me; it really placed me in a state of astonishment.

"The letter must state," continued the officer, "that Private Roger J. Morneau is traveling under my command and in accord with Order Number ___ and Confidential File Number ___ from the Canadian Department of the Army in Ottawa, Canada. In no way is he to be questioned on this matter by the military police or others in a way that could delay his train connections, or cause him any annoyances. Anyone having the authority to question the reason for his traveling outside of a military company may inquire of me personally anytime day or night. I may be reached by phone at these numbers ___________ and may be called collect."

After the secretary had left the office, the major turned to the sergeant and said, "You, sergeant, rush this man to the barracks and help him pack up, then drive him to the storage depot to store his gun and all the gear he won't be needing until he returns from furlough. After that is done, take him to the officer's mess hall and tell Lieutenant Brown to see that he gets a good meal."

He then looked at me, saying, "You might as well have an early lunch, as it will be a long time till you eat again in Toronto."

I replied, "You are correct, sir."

Again, he turned to the sergeant and said, "Sarge, make sure you have enough gas in your jeep to get him to the station without running out [it was a few miles away]. We can't afford to take a chance on having this man's good fortune change. Be back here to pick up his pass, and get him to the train station so that he will not miss his eleven o'clock train."

We then left and lost no time. The sergeant really took the major seriously. In those days, I used to enjoy a quick drive once in a while, but in this instance I felt the sergeant was overdoing it a little. After our return to the major's office, he gave me my pass, a paycheck, and then handed me a large and very impressive-looking envelope; it had a fine red ribbon attached to the flap tying it up.

"Open it up, and let me tell you why I have it this way," said the major. I untied the ribbon, opened the envelope, and found another one inside; on it was written:

SPECIAL TRAVEL ORDER
For Private Roger J. Morneau
No.______ Confidential File
Canadian Dept. of the Army
Ottawa, Canada

I then opened the envelope, and inside was the letter the major had dictated to his secretary earlier that morning. "I don't do this very often," said the major, "but here I feel it is necessary. To begin with, I want you to go first class on this furlough of yours. Secondly, because of the urgency of the times, there is very little travel being done by any private outside of a military company, and I don't want you to experience any difficulties. And above all, I want to treat you right. You are a fine young man and have been given a raw deal, and I am trying to make it up to you, as it is within my power. This material should place you in good favor with anyone having the authority to question your right to travel alone."

He then shook my hand and wished me a good trip. I, in turn, thanked him for his kind attention to my needs and for going out of his way to help me.

"Roger, it has been my pleasure to help you. In reality, I have never felt so good about helping anyone."

I did get to the railroad station on time, but didn't have a great deal of time to spare. The old steam locomotive was building up a lot of power, and the safety valve above the huge boiler was whistling at a high pitch. I had no more than placed my things in the baggage rack and sat myself down than the train pulled away. A few yards off was my sergeant in his jeep, waving at me with all the enthusiasm he could muster.

It all seemed to me a dream. What an eventful past twelve hours I had lived. But after traveling many hundreds of miles, and having shown on request the authorization for my travel to numerous military police (MPs) in the railroad stations of Toronto, Montreal, Quebec City, Riviere-du-Loup, and on trains in between, it became very real to me; and I realized that indeed I was a very fortunate man.

Concerning the impressions made on military policemen during my travel, as I was asked to show proof of credibility, I must say that as I presented them the stately looking envelope, and they proceeded to open it up, only to find a second envelope with the words "special travel order" written on it, most of them wouldn't look any further; they would close it, tie the ribbon around it as it was when they received it, and give it back. But there were a few who were very nosey and amusing to me, because they read the letter and were trying to figure me out. One instance stands out in my mind above all others. One of the fellows kept calling me sir.

I was seated in the waiting area of Windsor Station in Montreal reading a magazine when two MPs approached me and asked to see my military pass and a written reason of travel. The place was loaded with people, and of course all eyes within hearing distance became focused upon me. I handed them my impressive-looking envelope, which was taken by the younger man. He opened it, took the second envelope out, and after reading the face of it, said, "Sir, may I open it?"

"It is your prerogative to do so," was my reply.

He read the letter, and as he was doing so, his partner had stepped back a few feet. His next words were, “Sir, may I have my corporal read this letter also?”

“It’s my pleasure to let him do so, please do.”

As he handed the letter to his colleague, the man said, “Why do you refer to him as sir, when he is an ordinary soldier?”

“He may appear to be ordinary, but I am sure he is a high brass in disguise. Read the letter, and I know you will agree with me that we should treat him with respect.”

Then they came to me, gave me back my letter, and inquired how far I was traveling, and offered me their private MP quarters to relax in at the station, if I would like to do so. I declined the invitation, and thanked them for their offer. We chatted a bit, and the younger man spoke last by saying, “Sir, have a good trip.” They left me with the impression that they had me as someone who had succeeded in baffling their imagination.

I was, in reality, discharged from the army in Longueil, Quebec (a suburb of Montreal), several weeks after I was sent on furlough, as promised to me by the military. The one condition attached to my discharge was that I would return to the merchant navy immediately. And in no way was it intended for me to have a pleasure cruise.

It wasn’t long after the great conflict had ended that I decided that sailing was no longer the way I wanted to spend my life. The dangers of war had left sailing a dull, uninteresting occupation. And besides, I had had enough of being tossed up and down by the powers of the deep, so I turned in my resignation. Part of it went this way: “I am sorry, captain; I have to give you the news that I am leaving the occupation of sailing. My big feet are aching to walk on something immovable, they want something concrete to deal with for a while, and I can’t see myself depriving them of it. In fact, I owe it to them. So I have decided to head for the sidewalks of Montreal. I am sorry, sir, that we have to part company.” Thus ended a turbulent part of my life.

Chapter 5

A Trip Into the Supernatural

Good jobs were hard to find in the big city because thousands of servicemen had been discharged from the service and were out looking for employment. I decided on learning a trade; something I could enjoy doing, that would have some creativity to it. I was not willing to take up a trade just for the sake of making a living. So I decided to take my time and make sure that when I decided on a particular choice, it would be something I would really enjoy doing.

Meanwhile, to occupy my time, I accepted a job working at the Windsor Bowling Alleys and Billiard located on Saint Catherine Street West. At the time, it was one of the nicest places in Montreal for that type of amusement. I was the assistant to the manager of the billiard room. The work wasn't hard, I met a lot of people, and it was a good pastime. I had not been working there long when an old buddy I had sailed with at the beginning of my merchant navy experience came walking in; we were delighted to find that both of us were still alive. We had dinner together that evening and talked about many things.

One point of conversation upon which my friend, whose first name was Roland, spoke about with great enthusiasm was his new interest in the supernatural. He went on telling how fortunate he was in having become acquainted with a group of people who were members of a society that communicated with the dead. He recounted how the spiritualist medium had him talk with his dad, who had died when he was only ten years old; of all the many counsels his dad gave him regarding the future. It was interesting to me to hear Roland's new supernatural experience, but the sum of it all gave me a weird feeling. And in no way was I prepared for what was to follow—an invitation to attend one of their séances.

With all the enthusiasm that had built up, as he was telling me of the benefits derived by his contact with the spirits of the dead, Roland went on to ask me if I would be interested in attending one of their séances.

"Maybe the medium could have you talk to the spirit of your dead mother. You would appreciate that type of an experience, wouldn't you?"

Then his enthusiasm abated some, because for a short while I was so shocked that I could not answer. After a few seconds of silence, he continued by saying, "You wouldn't be afraid of talking to the departed soul of your dead mother, would you?"

Somehow I managed to say, "I wouldn't be afraid, of course not; but I would like a little time to think about it, having never been faced with such a proposition before."

He looked me straight in the eyes and said, "Morneau, are you afraid? I can tell by the way you look at me, it's written all over your face. Man, you have changed a lot since I saw you last. I remember you as being afraid of nothing. Roger Morneau was afraid of neither people dead or alive; of neither heights nor depths. I recall the time when you and I were deckhands along with six other neophytes, and the first mate came to us and said, 'Fellows, I want a volunteer to go up and paint the upper portion of the main mast, tomorrow. Which one of you guys is willing to go up there? The height is not great, it's only seventy feet. But one has to have a lot of guts once he has reached the top. He has to get off the board he sat on while being pulled up with a rope, and lay on one's stomach across the top of the mast [it was two feet in diameter] in order to paint on the opposite side.' I admit, all of us fellows were scared to death to go up there, and were delighted to hear you say to the first mate, 'I'll go.' Talk about courage! Man, you had it. Now tell me, you are not going to chicken out on coming with me to our next séance, are you?"

I could not refuse. I said, "Yes, I'll go with you." Because suddenly I had to live up to the image of Roger Morneau being afraid of nothing. I was hooked. So started a new venture in which I saw myself unwillingly becoming involved with an unknown power. At first, I felt reluctant to participate in the séances and almost refused to have anything to do with it. But pride did not allow me to do so; I was in a critically dangerous position in which the fallen angels gained an advantage over me.

Week after week, imperceptibly, I found myself adjusting to the attending of séances, to the point that I came to look forward to the time when I could ask counsel of the spirits. It became a way of life for me, and it reached a point where I couldn't see myself living without the influence of spirit power in my life. Then the time came when I found myself involved in demon worship.

One Saturday evening, my friend and I found ourselves in a home where a visiting medium was to be an honored guest. We were introduced to some of the guests whom we had not met before. One couple in particular we felt very honored to meet; the gentleman, George, was a professional entertainer, a jazz band leader who was in great demand. The band played in the most elegant night spots. In the late evening after the séance was over, and some of the guests were leaving, this band leader turned to his wife and said, "Honey, what do you say that we depart, as the time is getting late?"

She was at the time conversing with the medium, whom she found most interesting. "Why don't you go home and get your rest, and I'll stay a little while longer and have the Belangers drive me home." He agreed with her suggestion, and proceeded out of the house about the time Roland and I left.

Once outside, George turned to us and said, "You fellows driving, are you?"

"No, we are going to take the streetcar about two blocks from here," I said.

"I'll be glad to drive you there, jump in." During the evening, the subject had come up that both of us had been in the merchant navy during the hostilities. It came about as the result of the spirit medium having conjured the (supposed) spirit of one of Roland's coworkers who had perished when the ship they were on was sunk. The spirit had passed on some very attention-getting comments to Roland, and all present were greatly moved.

As we entered George's automobile, he began asking questions about the danger of our work during the war. In no time at all we reached our destination. He then made a suggestion.

"Fellows, what do you say we go to a restaurant and have a bite to eat, and at the same time, you could tell me about your sailing during the war? That fascinates me." And looking at my friend, he said, "You could also enlarge upon the statements that were made by the conjured spirit." And he added, "It will be my treat. Then I'll drive you home." We accepted the invitation.

George drove to Saint Catherine Street West, to an area known by the natives as the gourmet restaurant section of Montreal; and suddenly steered his deluxe Lincoln into the narrow drive leading to the rear of one of his favorite eating places, then left the car parked behind a black Cadillac, saying, "Joe is here; he is the owner of the place, a fine fellow."

We entered the place and were greeted by a hostess who informed us that we would have to wait in the lounge till a table became available. As we proceeded to the lounge, Joe spotted George from quite a distance away and came over to greet him. Being informed that we were waiting for a table, Joe stated that we wouldn't have to wait, because a reserved table had just been canceled by a telephone call a couple of minutes before; it was ours for the asking. We followed the owner, who removed the reserved sign from the table and seated us.

The cocktail waitress came over, took our order for drinks, and informed us that we might have to wait a little longer than usual for our food to reach us, because the place was filled to capacity. George asked for a double of his favorite alcoholic beverage in order to pass the time. We went on conversing and answering many of George's inquiries on the subject of sailing and of our interest and activities with the supernatural.

A fair amount of time had elapsed until our food was served to us, and a second order of drinks had been consumed, which served to place George in a very talkative mood, which in turn made him willing to tell us many things that I doubt he would have mentioned under normal circumstances. For instance, I asked if he would tell us a little about how he became so famous in his profession.

"I don't mind at all," he said. "As a matter of fact, I'll tell you the real and true reason of my success, something my wife doesn't even know about; but you must promise to keep it in strict confidence."

We assured him that whatever was mentioned would remain a secret, cherished and retained with all the powers of our being.

"You fellows know anything about demon worship?"

"I do not," was my reply. "Why do you ask?"

Without answering my question, he asked us another one. "How long have you fellows been involved with sorcery?"

"George, I don't understand your question. What do you mean?"

"What I mean to say is how long have you been pretending to hold communication with the dead?"

"Not very long for me," I said.

"I see where you guys have a lot to learn when it comes to the supernatural. You both are wasting your time by going to those spiritualistic séances; don't get me wrong, it has its place; it's a good pastime for women, in that they receive some comfort from thinking that they are getting guidance in their lives through some departed loved one. You see, the reason I was attending the séance this evening was just to make my wife happy. I go with her a couple of times per year, to make her feel that I am concerned with her interests; that's the only reason. What she doesn't know is that I have learned to go to the very source of that power, where a person can get real action; demon worship, that is."

By now, of all George had said to us in a few short minutes, one sentence stood out in my mind. So I said, "George, you want to clarify part of the question you asked us a little while ago, how long we have been pretending to hold communications with the dead, what do you mean by the word *pretending*?"

He smiled, looked at his watch, and said, "It's too late to explain that one tonight, but let me tell you that you have not been talking with the dead." And he went right on talking about his personal success.

"You see, for years it seemed I was a failure in organizing and maintaining my own jazz band. But by the great power, I have obtained everything I had always wanted. Of course, I had to become acquainted with certain rituals that needed to be performed before the spirits began to work things out in my behalf." Then George's face lit up with a big smile as he said, "Recognition came to us overnight; without any effort on our part, we were discovered (though we had been there all the time) and recognized as one of the great bands in our field. Somehow, the news media got all excited over us. We became the talk of the town. We were spoken of by the great people of the radio world, and in no time we were pushed to the top."

George then took another sip from his glass and a puff from his cigarette, and continued to talk. "We have been in constant demand ever since, and money is constantly flowing in. Our fees are some of the highest in the industry, because we are in such great demand. People like to dance to our music. In reality, the spirits take control of us, or in other words, possess us, energize us, and in turn we pass the influence on to the people. They like what they get, and keep coming back for more."

George sat back, proceeded to light another cigarette, chuckled a little and said, "You guys have got to hear this; I had an interview on the radio about a month ago, and I really enjoyed myself. There were six of the great people of the radio world from Montreal and Toronto conversing with me. They were fascinated by everything I said. In fact, I myself was amazed over my instant presence of thought. I had never been so witty in my life. And I enjoyed the esteem, admiration, and honor they gave me; it almost reached a state of worship. In addition, they were trying to figure me out; and when we parted, they had not yet reached their goal."

George then looked at his watch and said, "Fellows, it is getting very late, what do you say we get rolling for home?" While waiting to get the check, George continued by saying, "My success is easy to figure out once a person understands the mighty power of the spirits, and the process involved in getting that power to work for you." Roland and I were amazed over what we were being told, and asked George to tell us more about that great power as we were driving home.

"Fellows, I am impressed to tell you of my experience because I believe you are looking for a great power to benefit your lives; and I know that you won't find it by attending séances such as we have attended this evening. You may to some extent, but not to the degree that I know the power. Let me put it to you this way, why do you want to play in the little leagues, when you have the possibility of playing in the majors?" My friend then asked George to tell us how to go about getting into the major leagues of the spirit world.

"You two," said George, "are truly brave young men and have done a lot for our country. Now, I am going to do something great for you. I will arrange to have you both attend our next spirit worship assembly." Then George, moving his eyes from side to side, and with the projecting of an air of indecision regarding something that needed to be brought out, there and then said, "There is one point I want to assure myself of. I presume you have no reverence for Christ in your lives, am I right? The reason I ask is that we can't have anyone there that has any loyalty to the Christian God; it could be disastrous."

We both assured him that we had blasphemed God and gone past the point of no return. "I became aware of the fact this evening," continued George, "because the conjured spirits seemed to favor you two above all the other people present. I hope my asking didn't offend you. I had to just make double sure that you guys are OK."

I then added that in no way could God ever be close to me again. One precious and beautiful truth I didn't know at that time was that God's love for sinners is immeasurable when it comes to those who have been deceived by the enemy of all righteousness. We may have given Him up; but He does not give up on us. And this applied to my life, because I had been deceived from day one when it came to understanding eternal realities and God's infinite love for sinners.

I was somewhat hesitant to attend a gathering of demon worshipers. But my friend, Roland, had no hesitation in doing so. He reasoned that we were going to hell anyway and burn throughout the ceaseless ages of eternity, so we might as well get acquainted with some of the folks before we get there. I kind of felt that George might never call us to go with him, because he was under the influence of his favorite beverage when he made the invitation, and probably wouldn't even remember in the morning half of what he had said the night before. A few days went by and, sure enough, we both received a call to be ready at 8:00 P.M. the following evening, as George would pick us up.

That never-to-be-forgotten evening began by George filling us in on many details pertaining to their secret society. He wasn't a fast driver, and seemed reluctant to pass streetcars in motion; we must have made probably a hundred stops on our way there. So we had a lot of time to converse as we drove to our destination.

One interesting statement made was that we should not be surprised to meet some of the great and successful people of Montreal, and he named at least a half dozen of the notable ones. I was very surprised to hear this, in that I had already formed an opinion in my mind that we were probably going to meet a group of tough-looking characters. But on the contrary, everyone was surprisingly well mannered, superbly dressed, and possessed a winning personality. They made us feel as if they had known us for a long time and we were part of the group.

The meeting was called to order about fifteen minutes after our arrival. It was very informal. About two hours were spent by people telling of the fantastic accomplishments they had attained by the workings of demon spirits. Mainly business transactions resulting in great profits to themselves, because of their abilities to use clairvoyance and powerful mental telepathy (energized by demon spirits) to influence people in making decisions that would be to the benefit of the spirits.

One gentleman told of how as an astrologer using divination he became a counselor to certain wealthy people concerning their investments, and was himself becoming rich. He explained how a demon spirit was at his side on all counseling sessions, giving him precise information, audible to him, but not heard by the inquirer, on how and when they should invest. He stated, "These rich folks have the means to invest; I have the know-how to make it pay off."

My friend was highly impressed over the man's account of his successes and asked if he ever worried about being cheated on his share of the returns. His reply was very interesting. "I counsel on a percentage of the returns on investments; as you are well aware of, the astrology bit is only a come-on. I have no worries; my familiar spirit looks out for my well-being. Let me illustrate. One couple tried to deprive me of my fair share of one profitable industrial real estate transaction. They presented me with a sizable check, and I felt satisfied with the accomplishment, until my familiar spirit told me to ask them when they were going to give me the additional amount of seventeen hundred dollars, which made up my correct share of the profits on that particular investment. The wife fainted, and the husband was terrified. He quickly explained that they had no intentions of cheating me and that the money would be in my hands within twenty-four hours."

After each one of these success stories, the individual would always praise, or give credit to, a particular spirit by name, and many times referred to the spirit as lord of his life. In the short time I was involved with demon worshipers, my observations were that in their testimonies of how spirits had worked for them, they often referred to the demon spirit as lord-god. For instance, one would say, "It was wonderful to see lord-god Beelzebub's power exhibited in my behalf on such and such a day." Or someone would ask, "Sam, how have you been since I saw you last?" The reply would be, "Real fine, thank you, the gods have really benefited my life in wonderful ways." Those observations were to help me later on, as I studied the Word of God to understand the true nature of the great conflict between the forces of good and evil, and in making a decision for Christ.

That evening, one individual impressed me greatly; he was a medical doctor. That physician told about the spirits giving him great hypnotic abilities and healing powers, including the ability to take away pain and to stop severe wounds and cuts from bleeding. After recounting some very fascinating accounts of his healing people in his practice of medicine, he excused himself to go down to the worship room by saying, "Will you friends please excuse me? I need to go and perform acts of devotion, so to be regenerated by lord-god Nehushtan; I depend on his vivifying power to revive and heal my patients."

The meeting was in progress about an hour when a latecomer arrived. He was greeted by a number of people, referring to him as Charmer. "Hi there, Charmer." "How are you, Charmer?" "How have you been, Charmer?" and so on.

As we were driving back home late that evening, I asked George about him. "What about that dignified-looking gentleman who came in late? Some addressed him as Charmer. Does his name have any particular significance?"

"It has great significance, but I can't tell you about him now. After you have attended a few of our meetings and you become part of the group, remind me to tell you about him. He is a fascinating individual. In fact, he is believed among us to be the greatest charmer, or hypnotist, that has ever walked the sidewalks of Montreal. By the way, fellows, I was delighted to see how everyone this evening took to you guys; it made me feel good to see that. Understand this, we are a closely knit group; in fact, I had a hard time getting the permission to bring you with me to this meeting. At first I was refused the privilege, then through the working of a spirit counselor appearing to our leader on vacation in the U.S.A., I received a phone call giving me the OK, and the way was opened for you to associate with us and eventually become members of our society. I'll tell you more about it sometime in the future."

I felt somewhat uncomfortable as I heard George talking about me, with plans projecting a certainty that I was going to become one of them as a demon worshiper. But Roland was overjoyed about the whole thing. "After a few visits," said George, "I'll have you come downstairs to see our worship room; I think you will find it quite impressive. However, it will not be possible for you to visit the worship room of the gods till the satanic priest is present, and only after receiving the approval of the spirits."

That became a reality three weeks later. At this moment I think an explanation is necessary concerning the house of worship. This account took place in a private home, a luxurious residence in Montreal, Canada. That evening, as we were visiting on the main floor, we could hear faintly, coming from the basement level, a sound that closely resembled the type of music and chanting used by the people of India in their devotions. Every so often, some of the people would leave and go downstairs, returning about thirty minutes or so later. All that activity prompted George to lean toward me as we sat on a sofa, saying softly, "Our worship room is downstairs, I'll tell you about it after we leave this evening."

About the Charmer; it must have been about six weeks after we had met the man when one evening as we were returning home, I asked George if he felt like telling us about him. "Oh, yes," was his response. "You fellows should hear about that fascinating individual. But first, I'd like to bring your attention to the fact that we are, generally speaking, a law-abiding group of citizens. I don't know of any one of us who wouldn't give the shirt off his back to help someone. And we never really take advantage of people with the powers that are passed on to us by the spirits. But in the case of the Charmer, well, he is somewhat different from the rest of us. It appears that he has a weakness in his character, and because of it, he has employed his great hypnotic power, or gift, in a way he should not have done.

I should say that he lost his sense of direction for a short while.

"He is a very sharp businessman, owns two nightclubs, and has been doing exceedingly well. And as I have said before, he is a powerful hypnotist; he can place a person under his spell, or hypnotic trance, in less than ten seconds if he or she agrees to look him straight in the eyes and relax one's mental activities for a few seconds; or in other words, quit thinking about anything for a short while. Having two nightclubs, he has a lot to do with show-business people that come and go. Most groups stay for an engagement of about four to six weeks, then move on to another area. We became aware that some of the groups would break up or lose one of their members after performing in one of his clubs. And the dropout was always of the female gender. About six months ago, the Montreal vice squad raided a very plush house of prostitution, where all the girls were found to have been former nightclub entertainers and had worked for him.

"You see," continued George, "those girls would never have found themselves in the situation they were in if they had not agreed to be hypnotized by someone; that person can never from then on resist that hypnotist's power." He then made a statement that was to stay with me forever. "Posthypnotic suggestions," said George, "are carried out in an individual's life by the power of a spirit, in reality possessing and controlling that individual's mind, and thereby a great many of the actions of one's life."

I was in the front seat with George, and as he was telling us that, I must have had a look of disbelief on my face, because he looked at me and said, "You don't seem to believe me, Roger, but what I'm telling you is factual to the smallest detail. What I am talking about is not kid stuff; it's serious business. A spirit can actually cause a person to perform certain actions in one's conduct with great enjoyment, that in times past, he or she would have turned away from with horror."

I was so impressed with what George was telling us, and greatly surprised over the revelation that demon spirits can control people through hypnotism, and the statement that so much good had been done for people through the practice of that science. "You are right," said George. "The spirits have benefited the lives of multitudes of people through that means, and in so doing have made them dependent on the continual support of spirit power, which will at the same time establish them as permanent members of the master's kingdom. It is wonderful that spirits can operate so effectively in the lives of millions without being detected. Therefore, it is very important that any hypnotist, that is, anyone having been benefited by the spirits in receiving that capacity, that gift, should use it with great discretion and avoid bringing disrepute on that great gift."

Chapter 6

Worship Room of the Gods

It was our third visit to a demon worshipers' assembly. "This evening," said George, "our leader [the satanic priest] will be present, having just returned from a trip to the States." He felt quite sure that the priest would look favorably upon us, and undoubtedly would have us visit the worship room of the gods.

As we came in, we were introduced to a couple of people we had not met before, and then began to chat with a few people who came to wish us a good evening. Shortly after, the priest came in, and as he was shaking people's hands and speaking a few words to them, he slowly moved in our direction. As he reached us, George said, "Reverend, I would like you to meet a couple of fine gentlemen," then he introduced us. We chatted with the leader for a while, during which time he surprised us both by some of the things he said. For instance, when George mentioned about our having been in the merchant navy, the priest picked up the conversation and enlarged upon it by mentioning the names of the ships we had been on, plus a couple of details known only to us. I must admit that it made quite an impression on us. He then excused himself, and as he did, mentioned that he would appreciate having a short talk with us before the evening was over.

Not only were we impressed by what he said, but his very presence reflected an air of mystery. His piercing eyes, his bald head, his deep, low voice accompanied by a few chuckles here and there as he talked, not to mention his physical frame, his size alone was impressive. To convey a picture of him, I would say that he was in comparison, equal in size to the late General Charles de Gaulle.

After quite a lengthy testimonial session to the gods, the priest again joined us in a friendly conversation. He informed us that the spirits had acquainted him with much concerning us, and had manifested the desire to benefit our lives by bestowing great gifts upon us. When most people had left, he invited us to visit the worship room of the gods. To better understand the startling and almost shocking revelations that I was soon to receive, I feel it is necessary for me to tell of the mental image my Catholic upbringing had established in my mind concerning the devil and his fallen angels.

As a child, I was taught that the devil and his angels are in hell, in the middle of the earth, attending to the never-ending task of imposing various types of tortures upon the souls of the people that had died in a state of mortal sin. Demons were represented to us children as being half human half animal, having horns and hoofs and breathing out fire. As I came into my teens, I reasoned that the whole idea was so ridiculous that most likely it was an invention of some overactive mind, from centuries past, wanting to exploit the superstitious and uneducated. I questioned the existence of such beings as the devil and his angels.

We preceded downstairs to a very large room, beautifully furnished, undoubtedly the work of highly skilled interior designers and decorators. From the carpeting that pampered one's feet, to the soft piped-in music that captivated the ear, all was intended to fascinate the senses. But above all that was attention getting, I believe that the abundance of beautiful oil paintings arrested my attention the most. There must have been about seventy-five paintings, of around forty-eight by thirty inches in dimension, hung on the walls.

The satanic priest mentioned that if we had any questions, he would be happy to answer them. So I said, "Who are the noble-looking individuals portrayed in those paintings?"

He answered in these words: "Those noble-looking beings are the gods you have heard folks talk about in testimonial sessions. They are chief counselors, ruling over legions of spirits. They have materialized, were photographed, and then we had paintings made of them. They are deserving of great honor; that is why, right below each painting, there is a small altar making it possible for people in their devotions, to burn candles, incense, and perform rituals as requested of the spirits."

As we moved slowly along, we came to an altar upon which stood a staff with a serpent coiled around it made of brass. The priest made mention that the altar was dedicated to the god Nehushtan, whose power was so wonderfully put to work through the physician whose testimony we had heard earlier. Another comment made by the priest that didn't impress me very much at the time, but took on greater meaning as I became a Bible student, was that great miracles were performed by the god of brass for the children of Israel when they burned incense before the brazen serpent that Moses had made a few centuries earlier (2 Kings 18:4).

At the end of the room was a very large altar with a life-sized painting of a majestic-looking person above it. My friend inquired, "Who is this altar dedicated to?"

The priest replied, "It is dedicated to the master of us all."

Then I said, "What do you call him?"

His face took on an expression of pride as he said, "god with us."

He had referred to the fallen Lucifer. Today, as I recall that painting to mind, having stood there many times admiring it over a period of three months, I must say that the individual portrayed there had features that reflected a superior intellect; a high forehead, piercing eyes, the way he stood, that posture gave one the impression of being a person of action, possessing the dignity of a great general.

The answer of the satanic priest to my question was not what I had expected, and it was not really clear. Thoughts entered my mind. *Surely, he couldn't be referring to Christ Jesus. No, no, it couldn't be. But could it be that he is applying that name to the master of demon spirits? Could it be? I believe that's what he means.* So I asked, "Do you mean to say that this painting is a true image of Satan?"

His reply was impressive. "Yes, it is, and you probably wonder where the hideous animallike characteristics have gone." He chuckled and added in between chuckles, "Pardon me for laughing a bit at this time. Please believe me, I am not laughing at you gentlemen over your bewildered state of mind. I am in reality delighted and amused at the thought that demon spirits have been so clever in concealing their true identity that, even in this age of scientific advancement and great learning, a vast majority of Christians still believe in the 'horn and hoof' theory."

Then his facial expression changed to reflect an air of deep concern as he said, "It is most solemnly important today that the up-and-coming generation be led to believe that the master and his spirit associates do not really exist; for only in this way will they be able to rule the inhabitants of this planet successfully for the decades just before us. For those will be the greatest in importance as pertaining to the history of man." Then his facial expression changed to project a sense of confidence as he said, "Nothing is as intriguing to the spirits as to devise ways of causing humans to walk in a direction that will make them members of Satan's coming kingdom."

We proceeded walking slowly, looking at various altars and paintings, with the high priest explaining to us that demon spirits are in reality specialists in various fields of activity; they have a background of experiences that is measured in millenniums. They are engaged in a fierce conflict for the control of the minds of people, against the forces from above. When asked by my friend why so much effort was being put forth by demon spirits in deceiving humans, a unique answer was given by the priest.

He stated that everyone who can be made to disqualify oneself from being a member of Christ's kingdom automatically becomes a member of Satan's great kingdom, which he will before long establish on the earth. Those that go down to the grave while lead by the spirit of Satan, he will someday restore to life. "Christ and his followers," he said, "intend to bring an end to the great conflict between the two great forces by raining fire from heaven upon us, but it will not hurt us because demon spirits are now able to control fire so it has no power to burn humans." And he added, "If you doubt what I am saying, go to India or other areas of the world where the black arts have been practiced to a science, and you will behold fire walkers stepping across a bed of fire without so much as singeing a hair of their legs."

As we left the worship room, I expressed the fact that in reality I was very confused regarding Satan and his angels, and that I would appreciate any additional information that could reinforce what then appeared to be reality on the subject, versus the teaching of my Catholic upbringing, that Satan and his angels are in hell with the souls of people who have died in the state of mortal sin. The satanic priest agreed to take time and give us what he called a true picture of things. He went at it in this manner.

"Gentlemen, I realize that your visiting our worship room has raised questions in your minds that need to be answered at once. First, let me tell you that we, the members of our secret society here in Montreal, are the elite of spirit worshipers. When the great conflict between the forces from above and the forces of our great master is over, and his kingdom is permanently established on this planet, we will be given positions of great authority and honor. We will be richly rewarded for having sided willfully with what now appears to be the underdog, if you get what I mean.

"Our great master [Satan] millenniums ago had jurisdiction over countless numbers of beings in a vast universe. He became misunderstood, and was forced to flee his domain along with other spirits who sympathized with him. The inhabitants of this planet welcomed our master with kind understanding. And because of his superior intellect, he was able to become the rightful possessor of the planet by causing the original owners to forfeit their right to it by believing something that he said that was not in reality factual. Some people may call this deception, but in reality it is following the law of self-survival, which is a natural instinct in all great leaders.

"After it became known that the great rival Christ would come to this planet, taking the nature of man, to draw all men to himself, our master and his chief counselors decided to follow a strategy similar to the one that had enabled them to acquire their new dominion. This course of action would demand great diligence on the part of all demon spirits, in the counseling of humans to rule their lives in a way to disqualify them from becoming members of Christ's kingdom. The spirits' work would be to cause people to rule their lives by listening to their feelings, instead of the word of Christ and his prophets. In no surer way could demon spirits obtain control of people's lives without individuals realizing that it is so. In this way, all kinds of erroneous doctrines and ideas could be suggested by spirits, and humans would readily accept them because they felt strongly about them; regardless of what others would say about it."

By then it became clear to me that my whole ancestry had been victimized by heartless beings. The high priest, with his face radiating a sense of great fascination concerning what he had just told us, asked for the permission to take a few additional minutes of our time to illustrate what he had talked about. Having assured him of our deep interest in what he had just brought to our attention, and of our desire to know more about the activities of demon spirits, he continued his discourse.

"If you recall, gentlemen, Solomon, king of Israel, had been gifted with great wisdom, and arrested the attention of all great rulers of earth. At the same time, our great master became very concerned over Solomon getting all that attention and decided that a supreme effort should be made to control the entire world. Up to then, he had succeeded in establishing idolatry in every part of the world, except in the nation of Israel. So, it was decided that certain evil counselors [evil spirits] should apply their efforts to first cause Solomon to think highly of himself. Secondly, he should be made to feel strongly that it would be in the best interest of the nation to form alliances with surrounding heathen nations, even though many of the elders of his nation would advise him not to do so.

"No use saying any more but that our master's plan was a huge success; and when the day came that by Solomon's example the children of Israel were lead to worship Ashtoreth, the goddess of the Zidonians; Chemosh, the god of the Moabites; and Milcom, the god of the children of Ammon [names that I would recognize in the not too distant future as I read the Bible (1 Kings 11:33)], when they prostrated themselves before idols representing demon spirits, our master felt that his triumph was complete. He had reached his great objective; the whole world was in reality at his command.

"Gentlemen, I believe that by now you realize the master's great wisdom and cleverness in concealing his true identity, and thus assure himself and his dedicated agents that their diligence will be rewarded some day in seeing the generations of earth standing before them in humble obedience, acknowledging that their master is in reality a great god."

Having heard that account from the satanic priest, we were indeed impressed with Satan's wisdom and cleverness; and a whole new mental image of eternal realities began to form before my mind. But unknown to me then was that Christ, the Lord of glory, was soon to cross my path and arrest my attention, causing me to have a true revelation of eternal realities by studying the Bible with a young man, resulting in the completion of twenty-eight Bible studies in the short time space of one week.

After conversing a short while, the satanic priest added, "Do you have any more questions, gentlemen?" While we had been looking at the painting of the fallen cherubim, I had observed that Satan's altar was what seemed to be one solid block of marble, approximately nine feet in length, thirty-six inches in height, and about thirty inches wide.

I couldn't help but ask, "The master's altar appears to be one solid block of marble; if so, would you explain to us how something so heavy could have been brought down to the lower floor?"

The priest smiled and said, "You are very observant, Mr. Morneau; or, could it be that the master has impressed your mind to make that observation, so he can reveal to you his great power? By the way, young men, I have been told by one of the spirit counselors that the master has a very special purpose for the lives of both of you. So let me tell you of the spirits' powers. But first, do you mind if I light a cigar?"

"Not at all, sir, feel free to do so," was our reply. We were at the time sitting on sofas by a dual picture window, which gave us a beautiful view of the city bathed in a sea of light. I got the impression that the priest was enjoying himself greatly in telling us about the main interest of his life—the working of demon spirits—and we had the time to listen.

"The master's altar was brought to its present location in the same manner and by the same power employed by Druid priests in centuries past to erect the structure of Stonehenge; spirit power, or in other words, it was done by the process of levitation. As a priest, I have been given revelations by the spirits on the great accomplishments of Druid priests among the Celts in France, England, and Ireland more than twenty-eight centuries ago. I was shown that during the hours of noon and midnight, in the light of the full moon, the Druids were able to get blocks of sandstone weighing as much as twenty-eight tons to levitate into a precise position, and thus were erected their places of worship." He then took a couple of puffs of his Churchill cigar, sat back, and continued his discourse.

"Having been made aware of their accomplishments, I felt that the same privilege was mine to exercise and enjoy. I made my people aware of my intentions of giving the master a token of our affections in a beautiful altar. They felt that if I had the faith to believe that the spirits would see to it that the altar is set in its designated place, they would take care of the cost and transportation to the rear entrance of our place of worship. Without hesitation, I told them to place an order for an altar made of white Carrara marble; nothing is too good for the master.

"I knew by experience that the spirits' power is without limit when it comes to working for those who believe the word of the master. And my faith was greatly rewarded when on the first hour of November first of that year, the gods performed during our midnight devotional service the great task of causing that altar made of white Carrara marble to levitate and slowly come to rest in its present location.

"By the way, gentlemen, you have been greatly honored this evening, although you may not be aware of it. As we stood by the master's altar looking at that beautiful painting, which is in reality but a faint expression of his beauty and glory, the master appeared to me and stood by the far end of the altar for about three minutes, listening to us talk. That is why I suggested that we bow in the manner that we did at that time. Your complying with my request as you did brought great joy to the master's heart; I could tell.

"This may be of some interest to you, the master's presence has not been witnessed in our midst that I know of for almost three months because the United Nations are fashioning peace plans for the nations of earth, which is requiring the master's undivided attention; a work that he dares not commit the leadership of to anyone else. Peace on earth is not in the best interest of the master's kingdom; so he has the mammoth task of delegating to his legions of spirit agents many varied courses of actions that they must follow in order to perplex and keep personal feelings running high among the leaders of earth. In this way, problems will continually arise that will keep them searching for solutions to their difficulties."

All that I heard was interesting to me, but one point stood out above everything else. The statement that Satan's painting was but a faint expression of his beauty and glory. So I decided to bring up the statement for the priest to enlarge upon. Using the terminology that I thought correct at the time, I proceeded to ask, "Reverend, would you be kind enough to clarify one statement you have made; I am sure I have not grasped the full meaning of what you meant to convey to our minds." I then repeated his statement and waited for his reply.

"Yes, friends, the painting of the master is but a faint expression of his beauty and glory. When a spirit materializes, it deprives itself of that beauty and glory it possesses in its natural state of being. If a spirit would make itself visible to us right now, without shielding us of its brightness, we could not look upon it without hurting our eyes. For instance, while on my recent vacation in the U.S.A., a chief counselor appeared in my hotel suite in Chicago with the urgent message that the person I had left in charge here was about to wreck all the work the spirits had done to bring you in touch with our society; which I will tell you more about in the near future. His brightness was so dazzling that I could not look upon him. After giving me a few words of advice, he left. But the shock of that brightness to my eyes made it impossible for me to see correctly for about thirty minutes. A few minutes later, I tried to dial a phone number and couldn't make out the numerals on the phone; I had to dial the operator and ask for assistance."

Roland and I were very impressed by all we had heard relating to the so-called worship room of the gods. We conversed some more with the priest, who filled us in on many points regarding demon worship. And before leaving that evening, we were sworn to secrecy concerning what we had seen and heard. The high priest spoke words of incantation, parts of which we repeated after him, and we sealed the pact by depositing a pinch of powdered incense slowly above the flame of a black candle, causing it to burn intensely and fill the room with a rich aroma.

We were made aware that complete silence on the outside was a must in order to avoid bringing the spirits' displeasure upon us. On the other hand, our pleasing the spirits would result in many benefits to ourselves, as I will recount later.

After returning to my residence, I found myself unable to sleep all night. I could not turn my mind away from the worship room visit. I had a hard time adjusting to the thought that Satan and his angels do indeed exist and are actually beautiful beings, not hideous creatures. My Catholic upbringing had warped my mind so badly from reality that when truth was encountered, I had a hard time accepting it. About two months went by, during which I witnessed many supernatural manifestations of spirit power before I accepted the fallen angels for what they are, beautiful superintelligent beings.

Chapter 7

Spirits in Action

About two or three weeks after visiting the worship room, I had another opportunity to converse with the high priest about Satan and his angels. I mentioned to him about my expecting to meet a group of tough-looking characters before I attended my first meeting with them. He smile, chuckled a little, and said, "Spirit worshipers, like members of any society, vary in mentality, likes, and dislikes, and so on; depending on the national culture of a people to a great extent, it depends on the spirits' leading. In times to come, as you travel the globe, you will notice that among people where illiteracy is high, superstition prevails; and then the most degrading forms of worship are employed. The spirits in such cases take pleasure in leading people that way, because they know that it hurts their great rival Christ, who has claimed that if he be lifted up from the earth, he would draw all men to himself. They have proven him wrong over the centuries innumerable times, and find delight in doing so every day. Millions upon millions have gone to the grave without so much as having heard his name, much less believing in him."

While the priest was explaining about the intensity of demon spirits working in the lives of humans, I could tell that his emotions were becoming involved greatly in what he was saying. He got up from his desk chair and began pacing the floor as he talked. He folded his hands behind his back and kept looking at the floor as he went back and forth, occasionally looking up at me. The words mentioned here I recall clearly, because of the great impact they made upon my mind.

He continued, "As for us here in Montreal, we find ourselves in a way at the brighter end of the spectrum. Every one of us by nature was invested with mental faculties far above that of the millions inhabiting this great island. That is why the master has gone out of his way to acquaint us with the reality of things in the spirit world. He has a special work for each one of us to do; and stop looking at me as if you don't believe me!"

I was shocked by what he had said up to then, and undoubtedly it was shown by my facial expressions. I immediately replied, "Sir, pardon me if I have offended you by anything I have said or done; I do believe what you have said. I have much to learn in acquainting myself with the master's will, and all I have witnessed here in your house of worship is so new and different from what I was brought up to believe."

He then picked up the conversation by saying, "I didn't mean to snap at you, believe me, and you have not offended me. It's just that at times I take things probably too seriously. I was not boasting in the way I talked about our people here in Montreal; that was told to me by the master personally." By then the old guy was back in his desk chair, had lit a cigar, and was puffing away.

He went on saying, "Concerning you and your friend Roland, it was revealed to me a year ago that I would meet you here in our house of worship, but I had forgotten all about it. And as I have mentioned to you a while back, I was relaxing in a hotel suite in Chicago when a chief counselor appeared to me, refreshed my memory as pertaining to you, and told me to get on the phone immediately to the person I had left in charge while I was away; he was about to wreck all the work the spirits had done to put you in touch with us. I telephoned the man at once, and before I had time to say anything, he mentioned that George had asked for the permission to have you and your friend attend a praise session, and that he had refused him the privilege. Of course, I informed him of the chief counselor's wishes. Then I called George to tell him that it would be a pleasure to have you with us. As you can see, the master thinks a great deal of each one of us; so stop underestimating yourself."

After returning to my residence that evening, I experienced an almost sleepless night, as my conversation with the priest kept presenting itself to my mind. I didn't understand at the time what had prompted the satanic priest to burst out the words, "Stop looking at me as if you don't believe me!" And the thought of it all consumed my sleeping time.

Even though I had reached a place in my life where I had very few feelings for anyone in suffering or distress, and had no use for God, I see that the Spirit of the living God had not given up on me. And somehow, as the priest mentioned about demon spirits working at degrading humans in order to hurt Christ, suddenly I felt sorry for Christ; I felt a stirring up of emotions in the depths of my heart such as I had not felt since I was about twelve years old. A few words are needed here to explain.

As I have mentioned in a previous chapter, after our mother had passed away, my younger brother Edgar and I went to a boarding academy operated by nuns. It was a lovely place to be and everyone was kind, except one person. One of the older boys had been picking on my little brother every now and then, even though the nuns had tried to put a stop to it. One day, I found my brother on his bed in the dormitory sobbing away. As I questioned him about his sorrow, he said, "I wish our mother was still alive, I am very unhappy here; you see, if Mother were alive, I wouldn't have to put up with this one boy making my life unhappy with his unkindness."

I told Edgar, "I will take care of things so he will not trouble you again." My brother's words had somehow stirred up emotions in my heart over his distress that prompted me to take a course of action that could have brought me a severe punishment. I decided to beat the fellow up, even though he was bigger than I was.

It was wintertime, and most everyone was outdoors either ice skating or enjoying some form of winter activity. I went out, spotted the boy on the ice-skating rink, went up to the gate, and called him to come over. He complied with my request, and as he reached me, I immediately picked up a hockey stick that was nearby, hit the ice with a force sufficient to break it in two, and then proceeded to let him have a bit of what I felt was the right medicine. Fortunately, I was restrained by others or I would have injured the boy severely.

Concerning the feelings I had experienced when the satanic priest talked about evil angels degrading human beings in order to hurt Christ, deep in my heart I felt that same indignation arising within me that I had experienced many years back on my brother's behalf. My countenance must have reflected a sentiment that momentarily was felt, but not interpreted correctly, by the satanic priest. I thank the Lord that he was not able to read my mind or I would have been in great trouble.

One particular evening, my friend Roland had to work overtime at his job and was unable to reach me by phone before I left for the meeting. As he was riding the streetcar going home, he figured that if he went directly to the meeting place, he probably wouldn't be very late anyway. He then decided to transfer at the intersection of Saint Catherine Street and Saint Laurent Boulevard, and while making the transfer give me a ring at the house of worship. One thing he was lacking—the phone number; he had left it at home. If only he could remember the address, that is the numerals on the house, he could then get the phone number from the telephone operator. In those days, one could get that kind of service from the phone company in Montreal. So he took a small notebook he had in his pocket and pulled out his pen to write, but try as he may, he could not visualize the numbers he had seen so many times on the building. However, to his great surprise, as he whispered to himself, "I wish the spirits would help me," some invisible hand moved that pen with his hand still on it, writing not only the house number, but the name of the street in beautiful script.

He felt quite delighted over his accomplishment until the operator told him that she was sorry, she could not help him—the phone number was unlisted. About that time, George and I wondered what had happened to our friend. Then George got an idea, "Let's get help in solving our problem by asking Gerard the clairvoyant to locate Roland."

After a few words in incantation, Gerard closed his eyes, placed his fingers on his temples, and said, "I see Roland having just entered a United Cigar store at the corner of Saint Catherine and Saint Laurent Boulevards; he is now talking to the telephone operator. He wants our phone number, but is being told that it is unlisted. I will, by the help of my familiar spirit, transfer a thought to him [mental telepathy]. He has it, he is all set now; he is dialing. George, be ready to answer; he will be asking for you."

George started walking to the phone across the room. On the first ring someone picked up the receiver and after saying, "Hello," said, "George, it's for you."

When Roland arrived, he was delighted over his experience with the spirits. He showed us that beautiful writing on the paper and said, "I am going to frame this piece of paper; I have never seen such beautiful freehand writing in my life." Then turning to the priest, he asked this question, "I wonder why the spirit didn't give me the phone number as well as the address?"

The satanic priest spoke up, saying, "You did not ask the spirit for it. According to thy faith be it done unto thee." He then continued in these words, "The experience you have had this evening is child's play in comparison to what the gods have in mind for you two gentlemen. But you have to exercise faith in the spirits and expect great things from them. What is needed in your life is to witness the spirits' power and intelligence at work a few times, and then I believe you will be able to exercise a sufficient amount of faith so they will work for you in great ways."

It must have been two or three weeks later, as we entered that lovely residence, that the satanic priest greeted us, adding, "This evening you folks are going to witness a very interesting séance. An old acquaintance of mine is visiting our city; a fine gentleman, a great professor of ancient history, a historian in the fullest sense of the word. He has been affiliated with some of the great French universities, and his abundant knowledge of fascinating details of history has made him outstanding in his field. Or should I say the spirits have made him great, for they have supplied him with knowledge of the unknown pertaining to ancient history. This evening he will, by the way of a trance medium, uncover through the help of the spirits many unknown details pertaining to Napoleon Bonaparte's war campaigns. He is at present having his devotions in the worship room. Meanwhile, let me explain what is going to take place."

We proceeded to a sitting area, made ourselves comfortable, and attentively listened to the priest set forth the details of what should be a most fascinating séance. He continued, "A trance medium agrees to have a spirit enter their body, taking full control of their physical and mental faculties, and so be used as a means for the spirits to better communicate with humans. In such a session as will be taking place this evening, it has happened in times past that as many as six to twelve different spirits have entered the trance medium's body at different times, depending on the demands placed upon them. In a certain case, one particular spirit may be very knowledgeable about certain details on some points of history, but lacking knowledge on other details. In such a case, the spirit will refer to some other spirit taking his place, which happens to be very knowledgeable on that specific subject, having been present and involved with the events that transpired at that particular time. In fact, spirits are so precise in the information they give that in a case where a human once made a speech, or any type of verbal dissertation, the spirit is able to reproduce not only the words spoken, but the very tones and voice qualities of the person who did the speaking."

We conversed with the priest a few minutes, after which he left to go and check if his friend was done with his devotions. It wasn't long before he returned to tell us that all who were interested in witnessing the séance should go down to the worship room. The priest introduced the visiting historian to the assembly, and then asked for six volunteers to come forward, one of which would be chosen by the spirits as their preferred channel of communication for the evening.

The six individuals stood before the priest, who invoked the gods to manifest their great powers to us by having the spirits who were instrumental in directing and assisting Napoleon Bonaparte, emperor of France, in his military campaigns to reveal details of history when questioned by the historian present. A short ritual was performed by the priest, and while he was doing so, a spirit entered the body of one of the men and began to talk. The voice had a tone that commanded attention; the accent was that of a Parisian French.

The spirit informed us that he was a chief counselor, specializing in military undertakings, having jurisdiction over legions of spirits, and seeing that the subject being considered was of a very complex nature, two others of the remaining five men would be needed as channels of communication for the spirits. No sooner said than it was done. We saw the two individuals kind of shivered a bit, their eyes closed, and the spirits suggested that they be addressed as Remi and Alphonse. The eyes of the man possessed by the chief counselor remained opened but never moved, nor did his eyelids blink for a period of about forty-five minutes. The priest turned to the historian and said, "The gods are honoring your requests."

He stood up holding a clipboard and pen. His first words were of the type to flatter the spirits, by acknowledging that they had in times past given him information such as to make him one of the greatest in his field of learning. He conversed with the spirits for a few minutes, addressing them as lord Remi, lord Alphonse, and lord counselor. Question after question was asked, and without hesitation the answers were given.

At one point reference was made to a certain conversation between Napoleon and one of his commanding officers. The chief counselor stated that it would be preferable for Alphonse and Remi to reproduce the dialogue that took place between the two men, for the sake of accuracy in detail. It was amazing to observe; the voices changed completely, as if it were two different individuals talking.

I turned to George and said, "This is fantastic, what a revelation!"

George smiled and said, "If you find this impressive, wait until you hear the spirits reproduce the voices of people you have known, and have been dead a long time; that really blows one's mind."

The historian, having had all his questions answered regarding Napoleon Bonaparte's war exploits, informed the chief counselor that he needed additional information concerning a speech that had been made on the steps of the Montreal City Hall, by the former mayor Camillien Houde, just before Canada entered World War II. The chief counselor made the comment that he himself and his aides were unable to help him here, because their activities were all carried out in Europe; but that after their departure another counselor would take his place and inform him on what he wanted to know.

Again the men's bodies shivered, their eyes opened, and in their own voices they asked how long they had been instrumental in the spirits' communications. As for the man occupied by the chief counselor, he shook a little, his eyes closed and opened again, and another spirit said, "It is my pleasure to assist you in revealing the unknown. I was present on such a date of such a year, when Mayor Camillien Houde made his speech against the conscription of French Canadians into the armed forces. What would you like to know?"

The historian again stated his appreciation to the chief counselor for the continual guidance of the spirits in his life. He continued, "Due to the fact that no one was present that could make a shorthand writing of the major's speech, many different versions were given by people of what the mayor had said. Noble counselor, do you have any way of clearing up the matter for us?"

"I am glad to give you a word for word reproduction of Mr. Houde's speech," said the spirit.

Now, this is where I was amazed beyond my ability to explain. I could hardly believe my ears. There it was, a voice I was well acquainted with, for I had heard it over the radio probably hundreds of times over a number of years. Camillien Houde was a very controversial individual as a politician; he had no hesitation in voicing his opinions regarding anyone or anything.

In the late thirties, Houde was hot stuff for the French news media; all of his activities as a mayor of Montreal were constantly in the news. His speeches and comments were recorded and replayed over and over on the radio news, so his voice was easy to recognize. And now that familiar voice was being heard again, but this time reproduced through the agency of a demon spirit; and we listened to it for about twenty minutes. What a startling experience that was for me to witness.

Sometime ago, I was telling this experience to someone, and the individual made the statement that it could have been the departed spirit, or soul, of Houde giving the speech. I have news for anyone with this viewpoint; at that time Houde was alive and well. According to the records of the archives of the city of Montreal, Camillien Houde was born on the thirteenth of August 1889, and died on the eleventh of September 1958. So, like the demon spirit had said, it was a reproduction of Mr. Houde's voice and words. How spirits can do it remains a mystery to me, but they do.

That evening, as we were driving home, George stated his belief that when a person dies he or she is completely dead; and that when people claim to hold communications with the spirit of the dead, they are being fooled by demon spirits impersonating their departed loved ones. At that time, I found his statement interesting but didn't give it a great deal of thought because George didn't want to enlarge upon the subject, but instead mentioned that we should have the priest explain the matter to us when time would permit.

It so happened that on the following Sunday evening we were able to converse with the priest on that subject. He gave Roland and me an interesting account of demon spirits impersonating the dead. He kept illustrating the cleverness and wisdom exercised by demon spirits in their work of misleading humans. I got the impression that the man experienced great delight, some kind of devilish satisfaction, at recounting particular instances when great leaders were taken for a ride of deception by demon spirits.

The priest also made reference to three or four biblical accounts, but my having had no knowledge of the Bible at the time, it did not impress me; except when he mentioned as a masterpiece of deception the experience of Saul, king of Israel, and the witch of Endor. He stated how the spirits had lead Saul to rule his life by listening to his feelings instead of the word of his God. And how they completely separated him from the Creator by causing him to commit what was considered a great abomination in the sight of the God of the Hebrews, and by that means actually accomplished his destruction. He added in these words, "No greater glory could our master bring to himself at that time in history, than to lead the chief executive of the nation of Israel to bow himself before a demon spirit in the sight of all the inhabitants of the galaxies."

A few months later, the words he had spoken to Roland and I were a major factor in my deciding to break away from demon worship, by the grace of the Lord Jesus, and to accept and believe the Word of God in its entirety.

Chapter 8

Demon Spirits Pressing for a Commitment

One particular evening as we were conversing with the satanic priest, he mentioned that the time had come for both of us to begin exercising faith in the power of the spirits, because the master (using the priest's own words) had instructed him that we should.

"One of many gifts is yours to claim," said the priest, "if only you are willing to make an open profession of faith in the master."

That profession of faith consisted in taking part in a satanic ritual, in which we were to declaim before the assembly that we recognized Satan as a great god; the supreme ruler of planet Earth, willing to bestow great gifts upon believers. We would then claim for ourselves such a gift as we desired. The confession of faith would be sealed by depositing a pinch of powdered incense over live coals on Satan's altar, and then genuflect before it.

My friend Roland had no hesitation in doing so, and again I saw myself pressured by the power of association. Even though I felt like giving the matter some thought before making a decision, my friend gave many reasons why that evening was the ideal time to take that important step. I am ashamed of saying this, but I gave in and went through with it. I asked for the gift of divination, to be used in this way. In my sleep at night, I would dream of the names and numbers of race horses that would be the winners at a particular track the next day. Then I would go to a bookie and bet on them. That very first night I had such a dream; most vividly I saw the winners at three race tracks, and the action was shown to take place on the coming Saturday, three days away.

On the day designated, I proceeded to a bookie, and sure enough, up on the board were the names I had seen in the dream. As a shop worker, I didn't have a great deal of money to play with, so I placed a small amount on the first two races, and won about sixty dollars. The third horse was paying twenty-one to one; the reason being that he was far from being a favorite. But realizing that the spirits had informed me correctly up to then, I figured that I should invest twenty dollars. The horse came in first place, and I was the only person in the place to walk up to the cage to collect returns, a total of $420. I picked up the cash, said Thank you, and walked out.

Walking tall over my newly found good fortune, I proceeded down Saint Catherine Street to one of the many fine men's shops and bought myself a tailor-made suit of clothes costing about two hundred dollars. Similar experiences took place on Saturdays, and it wasn't long before the owner of the bookie had his manager bring me into his office; he wanted to have a chat with me. After conversing for a while, he realized that I didn't know much about the history of horse racing.

"I am amazed," he said, "over the fact that having such little knowledge of the subject of horse racing you invest your money so wisely. Do you mind telling me who feeds you valuable information?"

When he realized that he was getting nowhere with me, he said, "You and I have to part company, you are too costly to have in my establishment. You are getting too much of my money. I'd like you to leave this place and don't come back. If you need the addresses of other bookies in Montreal, I am willing to give you a list of them." I thanked him for his willingness to help and left.

That sudden prosperity was nice to experience, but in reality it didn't make me truly happy. Somehow it brought no contentment to my heart. Whereas my friend was having what he called the best time of his life, by the spirits working fantastically for him, I had reservations concerning my involvement with those folks; such as regarding the praise sessions to the gods. One particular evening, I had an experience that really went against my grain. After many people had given testimonies of what the spirits had done for them in benefiting their lives, the satanic priest suggested that we all go down to the worship room and have a praise session to the gods. He made one statement that really startled me.

"We will speak the language of heaven," he said. "This experience makes our master and the chief counselors very happy." His statement puzzled me, but I felt it was probably best not to ask how devil worshipers could speak the language of heaven. Once seated in the worship room, everyone was given a church hymnal, and I mean a Christian church hymnal. In fact, the priest mentioned three Christian denominations using that particular hymnal.

Talk about profanities and blasphemies being directed at the great Life-Giver of the galaxies; in my estimation there is nothing that humans could do that could equal this. After the satanic priest had performed a short ritual before Satan's altar in words of dedication to him, he told the assembly to turn to a particular hymn and sing along with him.

I will not at this time give the names of the hymns that were sung because they are sacred to me today, and writing the titles down while talking about that experience I feel would be a desecration in itself. However, I will say that they were mostly all concerning our precious Lord and Savior.

That must have continued for twenty minutes. While everyone continued singing, I didn't utter a word; I was almost in a state of shock. After it was all over and we were walking back upstairs, the satanic priest came to me, smiled, and said, "I noticed you didn't take part in our praise session to the gods. Do you mind telling me why?"

"Sir, I just couldn't profane those Christian hymns in the way you people did; the fact that I don't like someone is no reason I should sing profanities regarding his name."

He took up the conversation by saying, "I understand the way you feel, after a while you will adjust to this, and all will be well; it's like the first time a person witnesses a live animal sacrifice, it's a shock to one's mind, but after witnessing it a couple of times, they don't mind it anymore. By the way, we are planning to have you and Roland come with us to celebrate our high feast to the gods at a resort we have in the Laurentian Mountains. November first is a very sacred day for our people. I will tell you more about it next week when we meet again."

As we were driving home that evening, I asked George if he could clarify an observation I had made during the praise session. I had observed that after the people had sung for a while, some of them began to use a language other than French, yet the melody was still that of the Christian hymn. He explained that those individuals had become possessed by the spirits taking control of their minds, causing them to praise the gods (Satan and his chief counselors) in spirit language, thus enabling humans to worship them in a more elevated form of adoration. This type of service, he explained, has a dual purpose. First, the fact that demon worshipers are singing Christian hymns is in itself a way of highly deriding the name of Christ. Second, the act of demon spirits taking control of the minds of some of the singers and praising Satan and his chief counselors in spirit language, to the melody of a Christian hymn, actually constitutes the highest form of blasphemy against the God of heaven; and that pleases Satan exceedingly.

In addition to the above, my attention had been arrested a number of times by references having been made about live animal sacrifices, so I asked George to tell us about it. He explained that on November first such sacrifices are carried out by their people at a specific place in the Laurentian Mountains, but he preferred having the priest explain things to us. It turned out that it never was explained, in that the meeting of the following week was the last one I attended with demon worshipers. The subject never came up because our attention that evening was centered on an entirely different subject.

Unknown to me at the time, the fallen angels became aware that the Life-Giver was working in the affairs of men to shortly bring me to a position in life where I could hear of His great love for undeserving human beings, His great plan of redemption, and God's righteous character in dealing with humans. The spirits then determined to quickly pressure me into a deep commitment of faith. By this I mean commit myself to the spirits past the point of no return, as I will explain shortly.

On that particular Wednesday evening, as I entered our place of worship, I was far from realizing that I was doing so for the last time. As I shook hands with those friendly individuals who had gone out of their way to make us feel part of their group in order to please the spirits, it would have been impossible for me to think that just ten days later the same people would be changed into vicious enemies, planning my destruction, willing to spend a large sum of money to put out a contract on my life.

The testimonial session was very impressive, and after it was over the satanic priest had a short talk with my friend and I, telling us that the spirits were most anxious to benefit our lives in a very special way, and that on November first, just two weeks away, by making a definite commitment of faith in the spirits in a service of initiation into their secret society, the spirits would then reveal to us their plans for our life work.

As I asked the priest why we had to go through the initiation ritual before the spirits would tell us their plans for us, he explained that it was a matter of exercising faith in the spirits; and that without faith it is impossible to please their master, and that pleasing him would in turn result in many benefits to ourselves. He went about proving his point in this manner. "Gentlemen, please come with me. I'd like to have you hear how the master rewards people for exercising faith in him."

We proceeded with the priest to a room where earlier that evening, as I passed by the closed door, I had heard a fantastic clattering of typewriters.

He knocked, and someone responded, "Please come in." When we walked in, we found a man working at stuffing large brown envelopes with stacks of legal-size typewritten material.

"Julien, you have met these gentlemen before," said the priest, "but I doubt that they know your occupation, and how the spirits have benefited your life while you were doing good for others. So I brought them in to have them hear from you personally about your experience with the spirits once you were initiated into our society."

The man went on to tell us that as a young attorney, he saw himself destined to spend his life researching reference material for court cases being handled by a large law firm. But good fortune came to him when by the leading of the spirits he became acquainted with demon worship and his life was changed overnight. After initiation into the group, the spirits informed him that they were calling him to do a special work for those who had committed crimes against society and were not getting the legal help they should be getting to avoid spending time in jail.

He was to immediately start his own business, offering lawyers the unique service of preparing briefs for court cases involving criminals going to trial. The spirits would do most of the work. They informed him that letters had been sent to certain French lawyers throughout Canada, informing them of his specialty in the field of supplying attorneys with all needed materials to fight and win court cases, the likes of which in times past had been lost due to lack of what it takes to make their efforts a success. In no time at all, replies began coming in.

Next, the spirits told him all he had to do was to work in the house of worship every Wednesday to take advantage of their help. His efforts consisted in feeding paper into three typewriters until the spirits were done setting up each brief in its entirety. On the table in front of him were the typewriters and about fifty piles of paper. They were anywhere between one-half inch in thickness to about three inches. He explained that all that material had been typed as fast as he could feed the three typewriters. It contained the proper procedures to follow in court and also case histories of similar cases tried in the past.

When the priest asked him how his services were accepted, he declared that attorneys were just plain delighted in using his services because the results attained were so great. Again, the priest asked about how much money the work before him represented. He said thousands of dollars; many thousands of dollars. We chatted a bit, and as we were leaving, the gentleman invited us to come in and observe the spirits at work whenever we found ourselves in the building and he was occupied with his project.

The satanic priest was strengthened in his position of asking for a commitment of faith in the spirits, or in other words, to have us tell him that we were willing to be initiated in their cult. My friend gave him a yes answer, but I could not. "Sir, I am sorry to say, but I cannot give you an answer immediately; next week at this time I will give you a definite answer whether I will take that important step then, or at a later date." Not realizing it, I was shaking hands with the satanic priest for the last time, and then I left.

After going to bed that night, I was unable to get any sleep; I kept thinking about initiation into the satanic cult. *Should I go through with it or not?* The experience of the past few months kept passing before me, and many unanswered questions regarding the forces of good and evil placed themselves before my mind. Even though I had discovered many amazing facts about the supernatural, I still felt that there was a lot more to it all than I had been made aware of. I realized that demon spirits could not be trusted completely in the claims they made concerning what they declared to be God's unfair dealings toward them. Where could a person find truth? *Certainly not in any of the Christian churches,* I thought, *or I would have heard of it by now.*

In my state of perplexity, I felt that somehow I needed help in making an intelligent decision, and an almost overwhelming sense of helplessness caused me to exclaim aloud, "If there is a God in heaven that cares for me, help me!" Shortly after having spoken those words, I turned on my side and fell asleep. The next thing I knew, my alarm clock rang and it was time to get up. Thursday had arrived, and that morning I went to work buried in my thoughts.

At this time I need to mention about my work. Shortly after I had met Roland and began to attend spiritualistic séances, I had changed my work; an application for work completed sometime before had gotten me the job. It meant my taking up a trade of doing embroidery work for a firm that specialized in that type of service to the dress manufacturing firms of Montreal. During the time I was working my embroidery machine, I was thinking about the decision I had to make within a week. By Friday noon, I had come to the decision that I had no other choice than to go through with it. What I didn't realize at the time was that the Spirit of the living God was moving in the affairs of men in a way as to reveal to me, an undeserving human being, the Lord of glory's love and grace.

Chapter 9

From Demon Worship to Bible Study

At three o'clock in the afternoon, as usual a bell rang indicating the beginning of our fifteen-minute break period. As I was walking out of the plant, passing by the office, one of the owners, whose name was Harry, asked me to come in on my return to work; he needed to talk to me. As I entered his office on my way back, he was very pleasant, had me sit down, offered me a cigarette, and then started a conversation that seemed most important to him.

"Roger, I would like you to do me a favor; undoubtedly, you have noticed my walking through the plant this morning with a young man, showing him our operation. Well, I have hired him to work here; he will begin next Monday morning."

"Boss," I said, "that's interesting news, but what does it have to do with my doing you a favor?"

"Now, listen closely to what I am going to tell you. It's very important to me. Since he has left I have not been able to think about anything else but this: the man is a Christian but keeps the seventh-day Sabbath; and before taking the job, he mentioned that because of his religious convictions he would like to leave work at three thirty P.M. on Fridays and make up the time on the other days of the week, so in this way, he could prepare for the observance of the Sabbath."

"Harry, I am paying attention to what you are saying, but I'm not getting the point. What is this time situation you are talking about?"

"I understand that you are not acquainted with the fact that the Bible Sabbath begins at sunset Friday evening and ends at sunset Saturday. Being Jewish, I understood exactly what he meant and told him we would work things out to his satisfaction. I couldn't press myself to ask him what religious denomination he belongs to. Here's what I'd like you to do for me: I will have Cyril work at the machine next to you, and as you two get acquainted with each other, find out the name of his church and what some of his religious beliefs consist of. Don't let on that I brought any of this to your attention; be tactful, take your time. Even if it takes a week or two before you talk to him on this subject, it's OK. This really intrigues me, a Christian keeping the Bible Sabbath. I have never heard of it before today."

I felt an urgent need to set Harry right about the Sabbath and the correct day of the week to observe it. So I said, "Harry, don't you know that Sunday is the seventh day of the week? I learned that when I was a youngster in school. The nuns explained to us that God created the world in six days and rested on the seventh; but an error was made in the Gregorian calendar; in reality, Sunday should be on the calendar in the place where you see Saturday."

Harry smiled, pulled open one of his desk drawers, picked up a dictionary, opened it to the word *Saturday,* and asked me to read the definition. It said, "Saturday—the seventh and last day of the week." Harry then explained that the weekly cycle had never been lost sight of by the Jewish people, and that the Bible Sabbath is in reality the seventh day of the week, or Saturday as indicated by the calendar.

Concerning the Gregorian calendar, he admitted there had been a correction of time made, but it didn't affect or alter the weekly cycle in the least. It was done to correct the fact that ten leap years too many had taken place over a period of twelve hundred years. He then suggested that I check a good encyclopedia on this calendar bit, and let him know my findings on Sunday afternoon, because we had planned to play billiards together that day. I admitted to the boss that I was not very knowledgeable when it came to religion. I thanked him for making me aware of a very interesting fact of history and returned to work, having agreed to get him the information he was seeking as pertaining to Cyril's religious convictions.

The Spirit of God began to move upon my mind; as I was working, I couldn't think about anything other than what Harry and I had talked about. I became anxious for the hour of five to arrive so I could go to the public library and do a little research. Then I thought, *Why trouble myself over religion, what good will it do me? It's a waste of time.* But again, I felt a strong desire to look into it.

After leaving work that day, I went directly to the municipal library, where in a few minutes I had all the facts concerning the Gregorian calendar, and found that Harry was correct on the subject. Pope Gregory XIII decreed that the day following Thursday, October 4, 1582, should be Friday, October 15, 1582. The reason was to bring back the celebration of Easter to the time fixed by the First Council of Nicaea. The council had ruled that Easter should be observed on the first Sunday after the first full moon occurring after the vernal equinox. From A.D. 325 to 1582, ten leap years too many had been observed.

On Monday morning the new worker was introduced to all of us at the shop. "His name is Cyril Grossé," said the boss, "and he is an accomplished embroiderer; we welcome Cyril to our plant knowing that his presence with us will add to the credibility of our firm." He then walked him to the machine next to mine, telling him that the new machine should be a pleasure for him to operate. Then, turning to me, he said, "Cyril, meet Roger; you two should become good friends, in that you will be working on the same projects as time goes on. Roger, try to answer any questions Cyril may have about the particular work assignment. And if you fellows need help with anything, just call me."

The plant must have been in motion for about forty-five minutes when I began experiencing some difficulty with my embroidery machine. It kept dropping stitches, which meant my undoing some of the work and starting all over again. After repeating that procedure a number of times, my patience wore kind of thin and prompted me to indulge in an old habit I then referred to as calling down the saints from heaven. At that particular time of my life, that was a common way for me to relieve my frustrations.

After a while, I asked my boss to check my machine for maladjustments. He came over, adjusted the tension on the bobbins, and checked the machine for a number of things that could be the cause of my trouble, but it didn't help much.

At the ten o'clock break, Cyril and I went outdoors for some fresh air, and we talked about my difficulties. I asked Cyril if he could think of anything I could do to solve my problems. Cyril rubbed his chin a little, then said, "Seeing that you are asking my opinion, I believe there is. Roger, please take it easy on the Lord; I could hear your voice over the noise of the machines mentioning the name of the Lord, and I could tell it was not in prayer for help."

His answer to my question surprised me some, but it was put in such a way that it didn't upset me but still got his point across. I, at the same time, saw an opportunity for my getting Harry's inquiries answered. I immediately replied in these words: "Cyril, forgive me if I have said anything to offend you. I didn't mean to do so; by the way, I understand you are quite a religious man. Do you mind telling me what denomination you belong to?"

"I am a Seventh-day Adventist," was his reply.

"I hope you don't mind my telling you, but I have never heard of your church, or of its people. Could you tell me in a few words what you folks believe in and why?"

Cyril explained that the church's name carries the reasons for its existence. "Seventh-day Adventists," said he, "are dedicated to the proclamation of two great Bible fundamentals. First, the observance of the seventh-day Sabbath as the memorial of Creation, calling all men to return to worshiping Him who made heaven, and earth, the sea, and the fountains of water [Revelation 14:6, 7]. And second, Adventists look forward to the soon return of Christ Jesus, the Lord of glory, to this earth, in fulfillment of the promise made to the early Christians that He will come again to resurrect the righteous dead and translate the living who have been waiting for that glorious event. Then all of them, possessing immortalized bodies, will travel through space with the Lord to God's very own planet, where He is now preparing homes for those who are looking forward to that glorious event."

By then our fifteen-minute break was almost over and we proceeded back to our work. I mentioned to Cyril that though I had no real interest in becoming a churchgoer, I would like to hear some more about his religious convictions.

"Roger, it would be a pleasure for me to answer any questions you may have regarding my beliefs."

That particular October day was just beautiful, and a thought entered my mind. "Cyril, what do you say that you and I have lunch together outdoors; we could sit on the loading dock at the back of the building, and you could tell me more about your religious convictions."

"It sounds good to me," was his reply.

Getting back to work, I was amazed to find my machine running perfectly well. I began to think about what I had just heard. *The Creator of humanity calling people to remember Him as the Life-Giver, and to manifest their appreciation of Him in the observance of a memorial; very interesting,* I thought. The return of Christ to this earth and the resurrection, people possessing immortalized bodies, traveling through space to heaven, a real planet; the way Cyril talked about these things, he made it sound as if it could be a reality.

It turned out that the lunch period was the shortest I felt I ever had. We had the same amount of minutes, sixty of them; but because the Word of God was opened before me, in a way to solve the mysteries of my life in the way that it did, that hour of time seemed as if it were but fifteen minutes. The conversation went this way.

"Cyril, what you have told me this morning I have found very interesting; but it has caused a number of questions to arise in my mind. So, you want to try to answer some for me?"

"Certainly, tell me what you have in mind, maybe I can help."

To make sure that I had understood correctly, I began to review what he had told me before. "Cyril, you mentioned about the resurrection of the dead at Christ's return to this earth, and of people with immortalized bodies going to heaven, which happens to be a real planet. You stated that this would take place as the fulfillment of a promise made by Jesus to the early Christians. Now tell me, what happens to a person's immortal soul when they die, and what does it do between death and the resurrection?"

Having spoken that mouthful, I sat back against the building, took a man-size bite out of my sandwich, and figured that it would take a while for Cyril to struggle out of that one. He proceeded to answer my inquiry by asking me a question. "Roger, would you be very disappointed if I told you that you don't have an immortal soul?"

My reply was, "Not at all, but I know a lot of people who would. How do you explain that?"

"The word *immortal*," he said, "is found only once in the entire Bible; and the term is applied to God. Now, in all honesty, do you think that it would be right for you or I to take the liberty to declare that we have an immortal soul, after reading in the Bible that only God has immortality?"

I almost dropped my sandwich when I heard his reply. What a concise explanation! I was not expecting this type of answer, but what he said made a lot of sense. "Do you mean to say," I continued, "that when a person dies, he or she dies completely, having no knowledge of what goes on in the world?"

"Roger, you have spoken the truth; in fact, the apostle Paul in his Epistle to the Romans encourages all Christians to seek immortality; I am sure you will agree with me that the apostle would not suggest that we seek immortality if we already are in possession of it." I found Cyril's reasoning most thought provoking, making quite an impact upon my mind in that I had never heard words like these coming from a Christian.

So I said, "Tell me more."

He went to tell me that our Lord Jesus during His ministry on earth referred to death as a sleep. He stated the experience of Lazarus' death and Jesus' words to His disciples. "Our friend Lazarus sleepeth; but I go, that I may awake him out of sleep. Then said his disciples, Lord, if he sleep, he shall do well. Howbeit Jesus spake of his death: but they thought that he had spoken of taking of rest in sleep. Then said Jesus unto them plainly, Lazarus is dead" (John 11:11–14).

By then I was very impressed with Cyril's dissertation; in fact, I was becoming deeply interested and asked if he had additional information on the matter. He then reinforced his position on the subject by bringing my attention to a declaration made by the apostle Paul in 2 Timothy 1:10 that our Savior Jesus Christ has abolished death and has brought life and immortality to light through the gospel.

Those words weren't clear to me, so I asked him to clarify the statement. Cyril went on to explain that the fallen cherub and his demon spirits take great pleasure in confusing and misleading humans. And that from the day they caused our first parents to open the door of misery upon themselves and their descendants through disobedience, those evil spirits have labored following well-matured plans to cause mortals to focus their attention upon philosophies and vain deceits; for in so doing, the great blessings of God, promised to humanity, would be lost sight of. "Sad to say," he said, "but the plans of the evil one have met with amazing success."

I thought to myself, *Here's a man who understands the type of warfare carried on by his enemies.* "Cyril," I said, "please tell me more."

He continued. "The greatest blessing of God to humanity was to be fulfilled in the coming of the Messiah. Again, it is sad to say, but the children of Israel, the ones to whom had been given the oracles of God, became so confused and deceived in their minds regarding the Messiah that when He walked among them, the majority of the people rejected Him and one day shouted, 'Crucify him! Crucify him!' "

He then brought my attention to the fact that one of the most precious promises of God to humans is the resurrection of the dead and the hope of eternal life; but in the days of the apostles, the Sadducees, a learned class of the Jewish people, believed and taught the common people that there would be no resurrection (Acts 23:8). Also, the heathen nations surrounding Israel were steeped with the philosophy that when people died they entered a higher state of existence, so then the nations followed this by worshiping those who had died.

"We are to understand," he said, "by the declaration of the apostle Paul in 2 Timothy 1:10 that the teachings of our Lord during His ministry on earth, and by His great sacrifice on Calvary, have abolished death and overthrown all erroneous teaching on the subject. It is made very clear through the gospel of Christ that eternal life and immortality will be granted or given the righteous at the resurrection of the just, at Christ's second coming, and not before. And that when a person dies, he or she has no knowledge of time, but sleeps the sleep of death."

"Cyril, I realize that the Spirit of God has blessed your mind in a very precious way, making it possible for you, I really mean all Seventh-day Adventists, to escape the ensnarement of the doctrine of the immortal soul, which is in reality the most powerful deception perpetrated upon humans by demon spirits. Man, you have a lot to be thankful for." I felt like telling him about my affiliation with demon spirits, but figured that if I did, it could very well cost me my life. So I turned my attention to asking my new friend one more question.

"Cyril, I hope you won't consider me some kind of a pest, but could you tell me a little more about the return of Jesus and the resurrection?" The young man summed up his talk by quoting the words of the apostle Paul as found in 1 Thessalonians 4:13–18:

> "But I would not have you to be ignorant, brethren, concerning them which are asleep, that ye sorrow not, even as others which have no hope. For if we believe that Jesus died and rose again, even so them also which sleep in Jesus will God bring with him. For this we say unto you by the

> word of the Lord, that we which are alive and remain unto the coming of the Lord shall not prevent them which are asleep. For the Lord himself shall descend from heaven with a shout, with the voice of the archangel, and with the trump of God: and the dead in Christ shall rise first: Then we which are alive and remain shall be caught up together with them in the clouds, to meet the Lord in the air: and so shall we ever be with the Lord. Wherefore comfort one another with these words."

As Cyril and I walked back to our work, I couldn't help but express to him the deep sentiment in my heart. "Friend," I said, "you have a most wonderful understanding of the whole purpose of life; any person having this hope is indeed a possessor of great riches."

While I was making pretty designs with my embroidery machine that afternoon, unknown to anyone, my mind became a battleground for a fierce conflict between God's Holy Spirit and Satan's unholy spirits. First, I was made to understand why demon spirits have so great a hatred of the world's Redeemer. Also, why they have devised hundreds of theories to confuse and mislead humans; especially the idea that humans are immortal, and to back up this devilish doctrine, appear to people claiming to be the spirit of departed loved ones. Eternal realities opened before me in all their glories, and for the first time in my life I discerned a Supreme Being, the Life-Giver, being a God of love.

As those powerful impressions were being made on my mind, I also began to realize that I was a lost man. As I see it now, I would say that I have experienced in some degree what will be the experience of those who will find themselves below the walls of the Holy City, the New Jerusalem, looking up at the redeemed of the Lord possessing incorruptible bodies and joyfully facing an existence that will measure itself in millions of years on the earth made new. I can see that at that time the ungodly will say to themselves, "It is too late; I am made aware of eternal realities too late!"

As I meditated upon these thoughts, realizing that I was a lost man, and the thought of missing out on the glories of eternity, I began to perspire profusely, even though it was moderately cool in the building. I opened my shirt collar and rolled up my sleeves, but it didn't help any. I decided to go to the men's room and, as I recall, went in, locked the door, and in the anguish of my soul took hold of the toilet tank cover on each side to steady myself as I became quite faint with perspiration flowing down my face, while heavy drops kept hitting the water in the bowl regularly.

I said within myself, *It is too late; I am made aware of eternal realities too late! Too late!* I felt like shouting those words at the top of my voice, but I held back the distress of my soul. My hatred of God had now vanished; my godless life appeared before me and at the same time a realization of the fact that I was a victim of satanic oppression. The presence of demon spirits made to bear upon me in a sense of discouragement such as I had never before experienced, and have not since. That presence was felt physically, to the extent that breathing became difficult, as if I was being deprived of oxygen.

In my helplessness, I said within myself, *May God have pity upon me.* This was not meant to be a prayer, but to my amazement, the suffocating condition left me immediately, and also the feeling of discouragement. I then washed my face with cold water and returned to work. As I worked along, the thought entered my mind, *Could it be that the Life-Giver has heard the cry of my heart and rebuked demon spirits from carrying out a work of destruction? If so, why would He do this for me? I am a most undeserving human being. I have been a God hater, a blasphemer. In no way could God ever forgive me.* Yet the reality was that no one but the God of heaven could have delivered me in the way I had just experienced.

Another thought entered my mind that while I myself could not be forgiven of God and expect life eternal as it had been explained to me by Cyril, perhaps the Creator had in mind to use a worthless being such as myself to bring a blessing into the lives of other people whom He loves and wants to have in the earth made new.

Again, I couldn't help feeling that God had worked things out so that I crossed paths with Cyril, who knew so much about eternal realities. Yes, it could be that the God of heaven had heard my plea for help a few days back, when laying on my bed I said, "If there is a God in heaven that cares for me, help me!" *He cares; yes, He cares. That's it, God cares!* I almost shouted these words out loud at the top of my voice to every person in the shop, but I refrained myself.

Now, seeing that God cares for me, I should ask Cyril to tell me more about what he has found in his Bible concerning eternal realities. Because if God cares for me, a most undeserving individual, He must care for a lot of other people—good people who have not been made aware of what God has in store for them. I continued thinking, *If I concern myself with the eternal well-being of others, maybe God would deliver me from the power of demon spirits, and I could live the rest of my life rejoicing in the thought that even though I myself could not be saved, many of the inhabitants of earth could be made aware of the conflict behind the scenes, and be led to make intelligent decisions for Christ and for eternity.*

After a while, I began to feel great indignation over the fact that demon spirits had mislead my whole ancestry. I determined there and then that I had had it with the spirits; and I was from then on going to acquaint myself with Bible truth and work at cross-purposes with the fallen angels, so God help me.

After work that day, I told Cyril that I would like to walk with him to the streetcar and talk some more. As we walked along, I mentioned the fact that our conversation that day had led me to want to look into the prophecies of the Bible of which he had made reference to, the ones pertaining to the second coming of Christ, the resurrection of the dead, and so on. Would he be willing to give me Bible studies? His reply was that it would be a pleasure. Then he asked me a question.

"Would you like to begin studying this coming weekend, and then have one or two Bible studies every week thereafter?"

"Cyril," I said, "for reasons that I can't tell you now, it is very important to me that we begin studying this evening. Should we meet at your place or mine?" He invited me to his home for a 7:00 P.M. study. As we parted ways, Cyril had a surprised look on his face over my insistence that we begin studies that very day. Unknown to either one of us then was the fact that a week later to the day, we would find ourselves having covered a series of Bible studies totaling twenty-eight lessons.

Chapter 10

Monday Evening at Study

At the time indicated, I arrived at Cyril's residence. After introducing me to his wife and chatting for a few minutes, Cyril mentioned that he wanted to inform me regarding his affiliation with the Seventh-day Adventist Church. He explained that the time did not permit him at the shop to go into details on the matter. He went on and explained that he himself was not a member of the Seventh-day Adventist Church as yet, but was attending church regularly and had made plans to be baptized on the coming Sabbath.

Unknown to his wife, Cynthia, for many months he had been reading all of the church literature that she had in the house and in so doing had become an ardent Bible student. He had obtained a deeper understanding of the Bible in studying the Scriptures with Pastor L. W. Taylor, which had led to his decision to become a commandment keeper. Cyril suggested that Cynthia be the one to lead in the Bible studies we were going to have. I agreed that it was a good idea and bowed my head with my new friends while Cyril offered a word of prayer.

The young lady suggested that we proceed in our study of the Bible by putting to use a new study guide titled *Brief Bible Readings for Busy People.* Each study consisted of about fifteen to twenty questions pertaining to a particular topic of which the answers could be found by looking up a certain passage of Scripture. The length of time to cover a study was about one hour. Again, I agreed to the study plan, and we began with study number 1, titled "The Word of God."

It seemed like no time at all, and we had covered lesson 1. I was delighted over what I had learned concerning God's revelations to man. Lesson number 2 was about Daniel 2, pertaining to the rise and fall of the great world empires and the second coming of Christ to this earth. Cyril suggested that we should set a time to get together again for that most interesting study of the prophecy of Daniel.

Without any hesitation on my part, I asked if we could have that study right then and there. It was agreed upon and we proceeded. The entire study was great, but one verse above all others made a lasting impact upon my mind, Daniel 2:44: "And in the days of these kings shall the God of heaven set up a kingdom, which shall never be destroyed: and the kingdom shall not be left to other people, but it shall break in pieces and consume all these kingdoms, and it shall stand for ever."

After reading these words, I became deeply interested in knowing what else the prophet Daniel had been told about the establishment of Christ's great kingdom upon the earth. My attention was then brought to chapter 7, where additional information is given on the subject, such as verse 27: "And the kingdom and dominion, and the greatness of the kingdom under the whole heaven, shall be given to the people of the saints of the most High, whose kingdom is an everlasting kingdom, and all dominions shall serve and obey him." Cynthia mentioned that the words of Jesus will then be fulfilled as we read in Matthew 5:5, "Blessed are the meek: for they shall inherit the earth."

I was also made aware of the fact that the people who will be inhabiting the earth then will be persons who have been resurrected or translated at Christ's coming, just as Moses and Elijah, who are presently enjoying that perfect state of being on God's very own planet, located in the center of the galaxies and upon which is located the throne of Deity. Reference was also made concerning Revelation 21 and 22, where the apostle John was made to see in vision the earth made new with the capital city, the New Jerusalem, standing in all its beauty, with the glory of the eternal throne being established to stand forever on the planet where Christ the Lord of glory shed His precious blood for the salvation of undeserving human beings.

Words like those I had never heard before. They gripped my heart, and I wanted to hear more. "What is the next study about?" I asked. I can't recall presently what the title was, but one thing I remember is that the title of it awakened in me a desire to hear what the Word of God had to say on that particular subject, to the extent that I felt I had to somehow talk Cyril and Cynthia into agreeing to have one more study that evening. I lit another cigarette, took a couple of deep breaths, and made the comment that if Cyril would be kind enough to empty my ashtray, I could settle down for another hour of Bible study.

My ashtray was emptied and courteously returned to me. So I said, "Let's not lose any time; let's get studying so that you folks will not be going to bed too late." Their reply was that they usually went to bed around 11:00 P.M. "Great," I said. "It's just a few minutes past nine; we are doing well in our studies, so let's not lose any time."

I remember the reaction produced by my words as if it were yesterday. Cynthia looked at her husband with a look in her eyes that carried a large question mark, as if to say, Should we? She spoke not a word but just smiled and waited for him to say something. His reply to her silent question was, "I have no objections, carry on."

Meanwhile, I had nervously been puffing on that cigarette to the point that it was half burned. So I said, "Would you mind if I light a cigar? I am on my last cigarette, and besides, it is customary for me to reward myself whenever I feel I have accomplished something worthwhile; and in reality, this studying the Bible with you I believe is one of the most profitable things I have done in my life."

Without hesitation, Cyril said, "We would like you to feel at home while you are in our house; make yourself comfortable."

That I did in the only way I knew how—by poisoning myself. I put the torch to the tip, and the air in the room turned blue. I have a firm conviction that the Spirit of God had gone before me and prompted Cyril and Cynthia to sacrifice themselves for my well-being. They had an understanding of the powerful hold tobacco had on me, and decided to put up with the unpleasantness in order to acquaint me with the Lord Jesus.

Over the years, I have thanked God many times for the way that delicate situation was handled. I should like to explain. For seven consecutive days, we studied the Bible four hours per evening. It was not until we studied healthful living as presented in the Bible that I realized what tobacco was doing to me, and what those dear folks had put up with. And that took place almost at the end of the study series. When I asked them why they put up with my smoking, Cynthia explained in these words: "We enjoyed your company so, and when after the first evening of study you expressed the desire of coming back the next evening for more studies, Cyril and I decided that even if your smoking would shorten our lives by a couple of years, we wouldn't mind if it meant your studying the Word of God and becoming a follower of the Lord Jesus."

Now coming back to that third study of the evening, it seemed hardly any time before the study was completed. The Word of God was doing a work of opening eternal realities before my mind, and I could not turn from it. I wanted more of the same. So I asked what study number four was about. Having been told what it consisted of, I asked, "Could we have this fourth and last study of the evening, then I will let you folks go to bed?"

An expression of great surprise appeared on their faces, then Cyril spoke up, saying, "Why don't we plan for you to come back another evening this week and we'll have it then?"

"I hope that you will let me come back tomorrow evening to have study number five," was my reply, "that is, if I am still alive." I somehow felt that demon spirits might do away with me. I didn't tell them the way I really felt, but somehow they realized the urgency of the hour and agreed to cover that fourth study.

I think it appropriate at this time to explain why I felt that the spirits might do away with me shortly. Let's think back for a moment to that evening when my friend Roland and I visited the so-called worship room of the gods. As mentioned before, that evening we were sworn to secrecy concerning what we had seen and heard. The satanic priest spoke words of incantation, part of which we repeated after him and sealed the part by our depositing a pinch of powdered incense slowly above the flame of a black candle. We were made aware of the fact that complete silence outside of the organization was a must in order to avoid bringing the spirits' great displeasure upon ourselves.

It was sometime later, as we were attending what demon worshipers like to call a praise session to the gods, that the satanic priest went about explaining the great danger of anyone venturing out on a course of action that could bring upon them the spirits' displeasure. He recounted what he called a sad mistake made by an individual who had been highly esteemed by the master, and benefited in many ways by the spirits, but allowed himself to be disloyal in what some would probably look upon as something of little importance. It cost the individual his life; even though he lived in what was considered a fireproof building, the spirits burned the place down with everything in it, including the turncoat and his wife. George told us that he had known the people.

Another incident recounted by the priest was that of an individual proving untrue to his trust, and for about one hour the spirits terrorized him in his home by tossing everything in the house against the walls with great force, including large pieces of furniture, causing them to fall apart. The place was left in a jumbled mess. The man was hospitalized in a state of shock after his neighbors found him in his home. The man almost lost his sanity.

With those experiences in the back of my mind, I must say that Bible study time was at a premium. This explained the sentiment in my heart prompting me to press for that fourth study. The boldness with which I ventured out in studying the Bible under the conditions that I found myself at that time was not the result of human effort. But as I see it today, it was the direct result of having been fed the Word of God at that factory on that day. God's Word is life; its power is of the type that energizes a person even to the point of daring the displeasure of the prince of darkness.

So it was at that time in my life that the God of heaven had purposed that I should be made to hear the great truths of His Holy Word, and it became a reality. And in no way could demon spirits prevent that from taking place. At the completion of the fourth study on that evening, we agreed to resume again at 7:00 P.M. the next day.

Before leaving Cyril's place, I suggested that he read a couple of verses of Scripture and offer a short prayer. He opened the Bible to Psalms and began to read, "God is our refuge and strength, a very present help in trouble. Therefore will not we fear, though the earth be removed, and though the mountains be carried into the midst of the sea; though the waters thereof roar and be troubled, though the mountains shake with the swelling thereof. Selah" (Psalm 46:1–3).

Just as I was leaving the Grossés' residence, while my hand was on the doorknob, I thought of asking Cynthia what studies were coming up. One of the lessons was titled "The Nature of Man; State of the Dead." I said, "Good night," and left.

I said within myself, *I can hardly wait for the time of study to arrive.* But in reality, waiting for the time to pass was not my main concern. As I was riding the tramway home, the thought entered my mind that if I was still alive by 7:00 P.M. Tuesday, I would be a very fortunate individual. I really expected a visit from the spirits that night, against whose attacks I had in my own strength no method of defense. Yet I had no fear of dying. The Spirit of the Lord was blessing my life, undeserving as I was, for the sake of the Lord Jesus.

As I retired that night, the words of Scripture read by Cyril kept repeating themselves in my mind, and then next thing I knew, my alarm clock rang; Tuesday morning had arrived, and it was soon time to go to work.

To this day, the words of Psalm 46 have meant so much to me, for by those words I have been led to look up to God, who is the Fountain of life, the Source of all power. The One who is able to change, wonderfully change, the most hopeless discouraging outlook, in a way to deliver the helpless from the hand of the destroyer, and in so doing bring glory to His own holy name.

Chapter 11

Tuesday Evening: Studying on Borrowed Time

Tuesday evening at 7:00 P.M. sharp, I arrived at Cyril's residence. After chatting a bit, again we opened God's Word, having asked for the grace of the Spirit of God to bless our minds at study. The state of the dead was the focal point of our attention. I found the Bible to be very clear in answering human inquiries on this subject, regarding such questions as "Do humans possess immortality?" "Are the dead praising the Lord?" "Is knowledge found in the realm of the dead?"

The answer to question number one came loud and clear from the First Epistle to Timothy that only God has immortality; or in other words, man is fully mortal. Answer number two, "The dead praise not the LORD, neither any that go down into silence" (Psalm 115:17). Like a bolt of lightning, this scripture shattered into a thousand pieces the religious teachings of my childhood, leaving no doubts in my mind that in ages past some great artist in the art of deception had misled my whole ancestry.

The answer to question three began to reveal to me the love and justice of God in dealing with poor mortals. We found it in Job 14. "Man that is born of a woman is of few days and full of trouble. He cometh forth like a flower, and is cut down: he fleeth also as a shadow, and continueth not. . . . His sons come to honour, and he knoweth it not; and they are brought low, but he perceiveth it not of them" (Job 14:1, 2, 21).

After reading these words of Scripture, my heart felt a precious rejoicing in the goodness of the Lord. And I said to Cyril and Cynthia, "How precious is the reality of the assurance given us here in God's Word that our departed loved ones are neither in purgatory suffering, nor in heaven looking upon the distresses of their relatives on this planet in rebellion; but all are sleeping in the grave until the resurrection morning." They rejoiced with me in my newly found biblical truth.

The Spirit of God then made me understand that death is the complete opposite of life; that death is a state that can be reached only by a complete extinction of life. And my mind was cleared completely from the error that humans have immortal souls after having read attentively the record of Adam's creation as given us in Genesis 2. "And the LORD God formed man of the dust of the ground, and breathed into his nostrils the breath of life; and man became a living soul" (verse 7). I understood clearly that God's breath of life is that agency by which God vivifies and sustains these physical frames of ours. It causes the lungs to expand, the heart to beat, the blood to flow, and the limbs to move, and so on. And whenever God withdraws this life-giving element, life ceases.

I saw God's great wisdom and His loving care for the inhabitants of planet Earth, by declaring in the Scriptures that man became a living soul contrary to the popular unscriptural belief that man was given a soul, in that it closes all avenues for the fallen cherub and his demon spirits to mislead humans by appearing and claiming to be the spirits of departed loved ones who have supposedly entered into a higher state of existence. What a mind-broadening study that had been.

At the conclusion of the study on the state of humans in death, which consisted of many more verses of Scripture than here mentioned, a whole new horizon opened before me pertaining to God's character. I discerned the nobility of the character of the great Monarch of the universe as being exceedingly upright and kind. I saw justice and love walking hand in hand. I think it appropriate to say that I found myself falling in love with the Life-Giver. I became deeply impressed with the thought that God's holy character had been highly misrepresented in the Christian world. I realized that the Holy Trinity of God had been bearing abuses, or misrepresentations, brought upon Them since the defection of a third of the angels of heaven.

For anyone to understand and appreciate what I experienced during my Bible study time, one needs to imagine that he or she has never had a Bible, much less studied one. Life offers no real joy to one's heart; in that no sooner does one find anything to enjoy, then there comes the thought that death could end it all tomorrow, for eternity. An eternity of what? People with whom you have rubbed shoulders with don't know any more than you do, which in my case happened to be nothing of value. Then one day, in a most unexpected way, you meet someone who holds a Book written by the Life-Giver. Then all the unanswered questions that have entered your mind over the years receive an intelligent explanation, and more.

Returning to that Bible study night in late October 1946, I'd like to say that the study on the resurrection of the body, as written about by the writers of Sacred Scripture under the inspiration of the Holy Spirit of God, I found most amazing. After having covered the study of the resurrection and the second coming of Christ, we then took a concordance and looked up related verses of Scripture pertaining to those important events. Our study time that evening exceeded the four hours of the night before by quite a bit, and my hosts objected not a word.

Here are a few points of my discoveries quickly reviewed. For instance, I found that through the doctrine of the resurrection the Bible opens the way whereby all people can gain possession of immortality. Said the apostle Paul,

> Behold, I shew you a mystery; we shall not all sleep, but we shall all be changed, in a moment, in the twinkling of an eye, at the last trump: for the trumpet shall sound, and the dead shall be raised incorruptible, and we shall be changed. For this corruptible must put on incorruption, and this mortal must put on immortality. So when this corruptible shall have put on incorruption, and this mortal shall have put on immortality, then shall be brought to pass the saying that is written, Death is swallowed up in victory. O death, where is thy sting? O grave, where is thy victory? (1 Corinthians 15:51–55).

Yes, I discovered that Christ Jesus, the Prince of life, when He appears at His second coming with the heavenly angels, will give immortality to those who have made Him the Lord of their lives. Life will be restored to those who have lost their lives for Christ's sake, not only lost their bodies. The resurrection is the great event to which holy writers looked forward to as the object of their hope.

I was surprised to find that the apostle Paul, having suffered the loss of all things for Christ, was joyful over it, setting his hope in the resurrection out from among the dead (Philippians 3:7, 8, 10, 11). Paul's thoughts were continuously directed toward heaven. "Whence also we look for the Saviour, the Lord Jesus Christ: Who shall change our vile body, that it may be fashioned like unto his glorious body" (verses 20, 21). I found it interesting also that the apostle Paul, telling of his troubles in Asia and how he despaired even of life, trusted in God who raises the dead (2 Corinthians 1:8, 9). The apostle made no comment of his expecting to meet his Lord at death, as taught by modern theology; but set his hope on the resurrection of the just.

In searching the Holy Scriptures concerning the time designated for the righteous to receive their reward and the unrighteous their punishment, I have found it not to be at death, but at the two resurrections. These words of the Lord Jesus I found stunning. "But when thou makest a feast, call the poor, the maimed, the lame, the blind: And thou shalt be blessed; for they cannot recompense thee: for thou shalt be recompensed at the resurrection of the just" (Luke 14:13, 14).

I found that the apostle Paul kept his mind focused on the second coming of Christ, and his receiving personally from the Lord Jesus what he called a crown of righteousness. In the sunset time of his life, as a battle-worn soldier of the cross, his back carried the scars of wounds made by the lashes of five scourgings administered by the Jews (2 Corinthians 11:24). The stoning he received at Lystra had left permanent marks of the damage done to his hands, and still this champion of truth, who had been sustained through difficult times by the hope he held in the resurrection, though realizing that soon he was to face the sword of the executioner, raised his voice in a message that was to bring hope to generations of God's people, setting the time when all shall receive the reward promised the just, which is eternal life at the second coming of the Lord of glory. I was deeply moved by his words.

"For I am now ready to be offered, and the time of my departure is at hand. I have fought a good fight, I have finished my course, I have kept the faith: Henceforth there is laid up for me a crown of righteousness, which the Lord, the righteous judge, shall give me at that day: and not to me only, but unto all them also that love his appearing" (2 Timothy 4:6–8).

Throughout that entire study on the resurrection of the body, I had in the back of my mind the thought that if the New Testament writers believed that humans have immortal souls that go to heaven at death, they would surely make mention of Christ Jesus bringing them back with Him, to reunite them to their former bodies. Nowhere was it found, but many texts of Scripture proved the opposite. For instance, in 1 Corinthians 15, where the apostle Paul talked in length about the righteous dead and the resurrection, he talked a number of times about the people having fallen asleep and how Jesus will come and wake them up. What a day that will be!

My last point of discovery, and one of the most impressive to my mind on the subject of the resurrection, we read about in Hebrews 11, where the apostle Paul describes the faith of God's people in various ages. He tells of their trials and difficulties, of their courage, and how their hope in the resurrection and eternal life sustains them even unto death. He declared that they hadn't at that time received the reward promised to them; but will receive it with Paul and all the other Christians in that great day, when they will all be made perfect.

> Others were tortured, not accepting deliverance; that they might obtain a better resurrection: And others had trial of cruel mockings and scourgings, yea, moreover of bonds and imprisonment: They were stoned, they were sawn asunder, were tempted, were slain with the sword: they wandered about in sheepskins and goatskins; being destitute, afflicted, tormented; (of whom the world was not worthy:) they wandered in deserts,

> and in mountains, and in dens and caves of the earth. And these all, having obtained a good report through faith, *received not the promise:* God having provided some better thing for us, that they without us should not be made perfect (Hebrews 11:35–40; emphasis added).

What a wonderful Bible study that had been! What a revelation! What a beautiful hope! The thought entered my mind, *If only I could have this beautiful hope to live for.* Then another thought entered my mind that swept away that beautiful enthusiasm that had been building up. *How foolish of me to think that God would ever forgive me; His forgetting the hatred I held so long against Him, and above all be willing to benefit my life with eternal blessings reserved for the righteous. No, no, it can't be. That hope of eternal life, I better put it out of my mind. And there's my affiliation with the spirits. God could never forgive that. Forget it, Morneau, it's too late.*

It happened to be that the last verses Cynthia read to us to complete the study were those of Titus 2:12, 13, where the apostle counsels all Christians to "live soberly, righteously, and godly, in this present world; looking for that blessed hope, and the glorious appearing of the great God and our Saviour Jesus Christ." These words prompted me to express to Cyril and Cynthia my appreciation of the fact that they were graciously studying the Bible with me as they did. I also mentioned that I wish I could live with the hope of seeing the glorious appearing of the Lord Jesus, but my life had been such as to make that impossible.

"There is hope." said Cynthia. "We have a great High Priest, Christ the Righteous, ministering in the Holy of Holies of the heavenly sanctuary in our behalf. That beautiful temple is on God's very own planet, located in the center of the galaxies. He, the Lord of glory, came and died on a cross on Calvary so that He could be our High Priest; Him through whom alone we can find salvation."

I thought to myself, *If she knew of my involvement with the spirits, she would not say there is hope.* She continued, "There is hope for you, sure there is; there is hope in Jesus for every one of us. There is hope as long as one is alive to claim help from Jesus; there is hope, let me show you." She then turned to Hebrews 4:15, 16 and read, "For we have not an high priest which cannot be touched with the feeling of our infirmities; but was in all points tempted like as we are, yet without sin. Let us therefore come boldly unto the throne of grace, that we may obtain mercy, and find grace to help in time of need."

I grabbed the Bible from her hands, saying, "Let me see that." I really snatched the Good Book from her hands and read it for myself. What prompted me to snatch the Bible out of her hands I believe was the fact that the Spirit of God was blessing my mind with hope. And I grabbed for the lifeline of hope. During my days in the merchant navy, I had the occasion of tossing a lifeline to a man that had fallen overboard; oh, how he grabbed that line and held on for dear life. In like manner, in my lost condition, I saw a hope and quickly reached for it.

Because of the very late hour, I expressed the desire that Cyril offer a few words of prayer, and then I would leave for home. I asked if I could again study with them the next evening. To that they agreed, prayer was offered, I said good night and departed.

As I was sitting on the tramway car, with its wheels squealing, and the humdrum of doors opening and closing, people getting on and off, the conductor shouting out the name of streets ahead, I was looking through the window at the pavement. Nothing could get my attention even for a moment. My mind was totally occupied with what Cynthia had said. I could hear her very words, *"There is hope for you, sure there is; there is hope in Jesus for every one of us. There is hope as long as one is alive to claim help from Jesus, there is hope."*

Then a voice seemed to say to my mind, *"Yes, there is hope for the hopeless, there is hope for the undeserving, there is hope for spirit worshipers. There is hope for you in Jesus."* In my mind, I could see that page of the Bible with the words of hope I had read. Yes, it was verses 15 and 16, the last verses of Hebrews 4. I could see chapter 5 just below them. I said within myself, *I need to get a Bible. Where would I find a place to buy a Bible?* Well, the good Lord had also made arrangement for that. But before telling how I got a brand-new Bible the next day for $1.50, I'd like to show how the wonderful God we serve takes to heart our prayer requests and the needs of people who need His help but don't know how to ask Him.

After thirty-two years of not seeing each other, Cyril and Cynthia met Hilda, my wife, and me in Toronto, Canada. Those dear friends had moved to the United States shortly after my transition from the powers of darkness to the glorious hope found in the Lord Jesus, my Strength and my Redeemer. As we reminisced about those days of the autumn of 1946, Cyril made a statement that thrilled my heart greatly, in that in it I saw the merciful workings of the Spirit of God's love on my behalf. It concerns his decision to quit the job he had, where he was perfectly happy, and taking a job with the firm I was working for.

I asked Cyril if he could put it in writing so I could make it part of my manuscript. It reveals God's great power of love working through His ministry of reconciliation. I will use here but a short part of the testimony that Cyril put in writing for me. I will use more of his personal testimony showing the power of God's love later on, in a chapter entitled "Walking Under the Shadow of Death." Here are his own words:

> After several months of being married, I started to sit in on some Bible studies with Elder Warren Taylor, the pastor of the English Seventh-day Adventist church in Montreal. I had no problem believing anything Pastor Taylor said because all he did was quote the Bible just as it was written.
>
> Then one evening he gave the lesson on the Sabbath. This lesson carried

me back to that day in Halifax when I asked my grandmother about the correct day for the Sabbath, but I still was not convinced. That night, without telling anyone else, I prayed and asked God to help me believe in the Sabbath. I requested that God in His wisdom and holy power grant me the ability to convince one soul of what I now believed and this would be a sign that God wanted me to keep the Bible Sabbath.

The following Monday I started to work on my job as usual; however, I had grown tired or restless and I suddenly decided to quit my job. I had heard of a new factory that needed men with my particular talent, and that evening I went for an interview. To my surprise, I got the job plus a larger salary. I returned to my old job and gave them the required two weeks' notice.

At last the time came for me to go to my new job, and that Monday morning I sat down beside a new worker who had some strange habits. First he smoked like a locomotive. I was happy to be able to open the windows. His other habit was that whenever his machine failed to work, he would surprise me with profanities that were unbelievable. I had forgotten about my prayer to God, but God never forgets the prayer of His children. Little did I know that this younger man, who sat next to me, would that very day request of me, and even demand, Bible studies starting that very night. I didn't know the serious problems that filled the life of Roger Morneau as he sat working at his machine on that morning in Montreal, Canada.

I felt impressed to insert here Cyril's account of his changing jobs so that the goodness of the Lord may be revealed, and that we all may grow in the knowledge of the fact that the Author of our being, the One who formed us in His own divine image, is in reality a prayer-answering God. And that He can answer what we may consider an almost insignificant request, by turning it into a work of glory to Himself, and a superb blessing to some helpless soul.

That almost sleepless night of mine, a few days before I met Cyril, and that one-sentence prayer spoken in the wee hours of the morning, when I said, "If there is a God in heaven that cares for me, help me!" was anticipated by the Life-Giver, and He had prepared to give me the right kind of help.

When Cyril talked to God about his need of being solidified in the observance of the Bible Sabbath, and of his sharing the Word of life with a soul who needed it, the Almighty said, "Very well, I have just the person for you." Then His Holy Spirit moved into action, prompting Cyril to want to change his job. And when the pressure mounted on my mind in having to make what I feel was to be the most important decision I would ever have to make in my living days, God was there to help; His Holy Spirit had worked out all the details to perfection. And when I say all the details, I mean all in the fullest sense of the word. I am thinking mainly about my Jewish boss Harry and his obsession for finding out what denomination Cyril belonged to, and his asking me to do him a favor in finding that out for him.

Returning for a moment to the activities of the evening, I'd like to say that the Bible studies we covered served to give me a panoramic view of eternal realities. The Spirit of God blessed my mind with such clarity of perception as to eliminate the necessity of my having to delve into deep theological research, necessitating a long period of time to assimilate the matter in question. I was limited on time; I was in a crisis situation. Time was not mine to use as I pleased. I knew that a confrontation with the spirits was likely to take place before long.

I felt as if I was living on borrowed time.

Chapter 12

Wednesday: The Day of Promises

Yes, I had promised the satanic priest that on that particular Wednesday I would have an answer for him pertaining to being initiated into their secret society. The spirits were promising to benefit my life in a very special way, according to the satanic priest. But in two short days I had become acquainted with some of the great promises from the Word of God.

Wednesday morning I went to work thinking about promises, and what I should do about them all. It was a mind-sobering day. I did a lot of thinking and very little talking; a thousand and one thoughts presented themselves to my mind. By 5:00 P.M., I had decided to walk home instead of taking the streetcar. I had also decided to pass up the evening meal. I felt no need of eating. I was too tense to enjoy any food. I had to make a very unpleasant phone call to my friend Roland, to let him know that for reasons that I could not explain then, I would not be able to attend the usual Wednesday evening praise session to the gods. And for him to tell the satanic priest that I would be getting in touch with him before long.

As I was walking slowly north on Bleury Street, I passed by many various types of shops, not paying attention to any. But for no reason that I can explain, I happened to look at one window for a moment. I must have gone about twenty feet when it dawned on me that I had seen a Bible in that window. I went back and looked again. Yes, there was a beautiful new Bible in front of all the junk displayed there.

I can't exactly recall the name of the place, but the sign said something like Sam's Pawnshop and Bargain Store. Just back of the Bible was a small handmade sign that read: "This Bible on a great special today, come in for a real bargain." I proceeded to enter the place, moving slowly because it was loaded with merchandise of all types. Showcases were packed tight and placed in such a way that one could hardly figure out where to walk. Men's suits were on racks, guitars and all kinds of musical instruments were hung from the ceiling. Signs and more signs were everywhere, telling of bargains and more bargains. I became deeply impressed that I was in a real bargain shop.

A little old gentleman came toward me and said, "Can I help you, sir?"

"I am interested in the Bible you have in the display window. How much do you want for it?"

"Oh, the Bible, let me get it for you."

"Sir, you don't have to get it, I want to know the price because I do not have much money on me." He proceeded to get it anyway.

"You have enough for this Bible, I am sure; I just placed it in the window about an hour ago. I am running a special on it." He went right on talking, and I tried to be courteous because of his age.

"If you want a good price on a Bible, never go to a Bible store; always come to a place like this." By then he had managed to walk among all his junk and was coming back without having upset anything. I thought to myself, *This little old gentleman must have been an acrobat in his younger days.* He placed it in my hands, saying, "It's a beautiful Bible, isn't it?"

"How much?" I asked.

"You will not have to pay the high price you would have to pay if you went to one of those Bible stores. You see, a Bible like this probably sells for about fifteen dollars, maybe more, let me show you why." He opened the Bible to the New Testament, saying, "I don't know much about Bibles, but I know that one with the red printing, as you see here, is the best."

I was ready to ask him the price once more, when he beat me to it. "I had set my mind on getting a pretty good price for this one, but the more I talk to you about this Bible, the lower my price is getting."

"That's great," I said. "Keep on talking until you get to a dollar fifty and then I will reach in my pocket and pay you for it."

"It's sold; give me a dollar fifty."

I really didn't mean what I had said, and proceeded to explain to the man that I didn't want to take advantage of him and would be happy to pay an amount that he felt would be reasonable.

"No, I will not take a penny more; once I state a price, that is the price I sell for," said the man. As I was giving him the money, he said, "Of course, I won't wrap it up for you, at that price I can't afford the wrapping paper. You don't mind taking it this way do you?"

"Not at all," was my reply, and I proceeded out of the bargain store. As I was closing the door, I stopped, turned around, and went back in. A thought had come into my mind.

"Anything wrong?" said that little gentleman.

"Sir, this is one of the most unusual business transactions I have ever made. Would you tell me honestly why you sold me this Bible the way you did? You sounded as if you wanted to get rid of it."

He looked me straight in the eyes and said, "Son, this is undoubtedly a stolen Bible; I took it in last week with other items a couple of guys sold me. Up to then, I was having a good month in sales, but as I was thinking an hour before you came in, business has been no good at all from the time I bought that Bible from those fellows. So, I immediately placed the Bible on sale in the window. Take it, son, and go home and read it. God bless you."

As he said those words, I thought of Hebrews 4:15, 16, those beautiful words of hope. I said Thank you and left. Real joy entered my heart as I walked down the street with my new Bible under my arm. I hadn't felt like this since I was a youngster. I was headed to my apartment as I read those beautiful verses of Hebrews 4, about Jesus being my High Priest. It was as if a cloud of gloom had been overshadowing me, and it was now being blown away. In fact, I felt so good that my appetite came back. As I passed by a Jewish delicatessen, I decided to go and get myself a sandwich, and eat it at home while reading my new Bible in the time I had before leaving to go to Cyril's place for more Bible studies.

Something then happened that intensified my interest in the book of Hebrews. As I entered my place, I became aware that the time was passing faster than I realized. Quickly, I placed my Bible on my rocking chair and turned around to raise the shade on a window. In so doing, I knocked the chair with my elbow, which in turn caused the Bible to fall on the floor. I exclaimed to myself, "Oh no, my new stolen Bible on the floor!"

It had fallen right side up and opened to Hebrews 7. I picked it up and began to read the words of the apostle Paul, "But this man, because he continueth ever, hath an unchangeable priesthood. Wherefore he is able also to save them to the uttermost that come unto God by him, seeing he ever liveth to make intercession for them." As my eyes moved downward, I began reading again. "Now of the things which we have spoken this is the sum: We have such an high priest, who is set on the right hand of the throne of the Majesty in the heavens; a minister of the sanctuary, and of the true tabernacle, which the Lord pitched, and not man" (Hebrews 7:24, 25; 8:1, 2).

Through these verses, I heard the Lord Jesus speaking to me, declaring Himself to be a living, loving, and mighty Redeemer, able to save completely those who come to God by Him. And this included His being able to control the power of demon spirits, rendering them incapable of carrying out upon me a work of destruction that would have been their pleasure to do. Hope took hold of my heart; I was filled with admiration for my newfound Friend, the Lord of glory.

As I traveled to Cyril's place for more Bible studies, I read the entire epistle of the apostle Paul to the Hebrews. On my way back home, I read it over again. When I arrived home, I read it a third time. I was fascinated with the stories of redemption as spoken of by the apostle. His expounding on the Scriptures to show that the intercession of Christ on humanity's behalf in the heavenly sanctuary being as essential to humanity's salvation as was His death upon the cross made a deep impression upon my mind.

I saw the Lord Jesus as One who loves the unlovable; a merciful High Priest. I saw Him as One who is able to make all things right, being a specialist in salvation. I saw that the Lord of glory allowed Himself to be nailed to a cross that through death He might destroy him that had the power of death, that is, the devil. I understood that my only hope was to place my trust in the merits of the precious blood of Him who can save to the uttermost all that come unto God by Him.

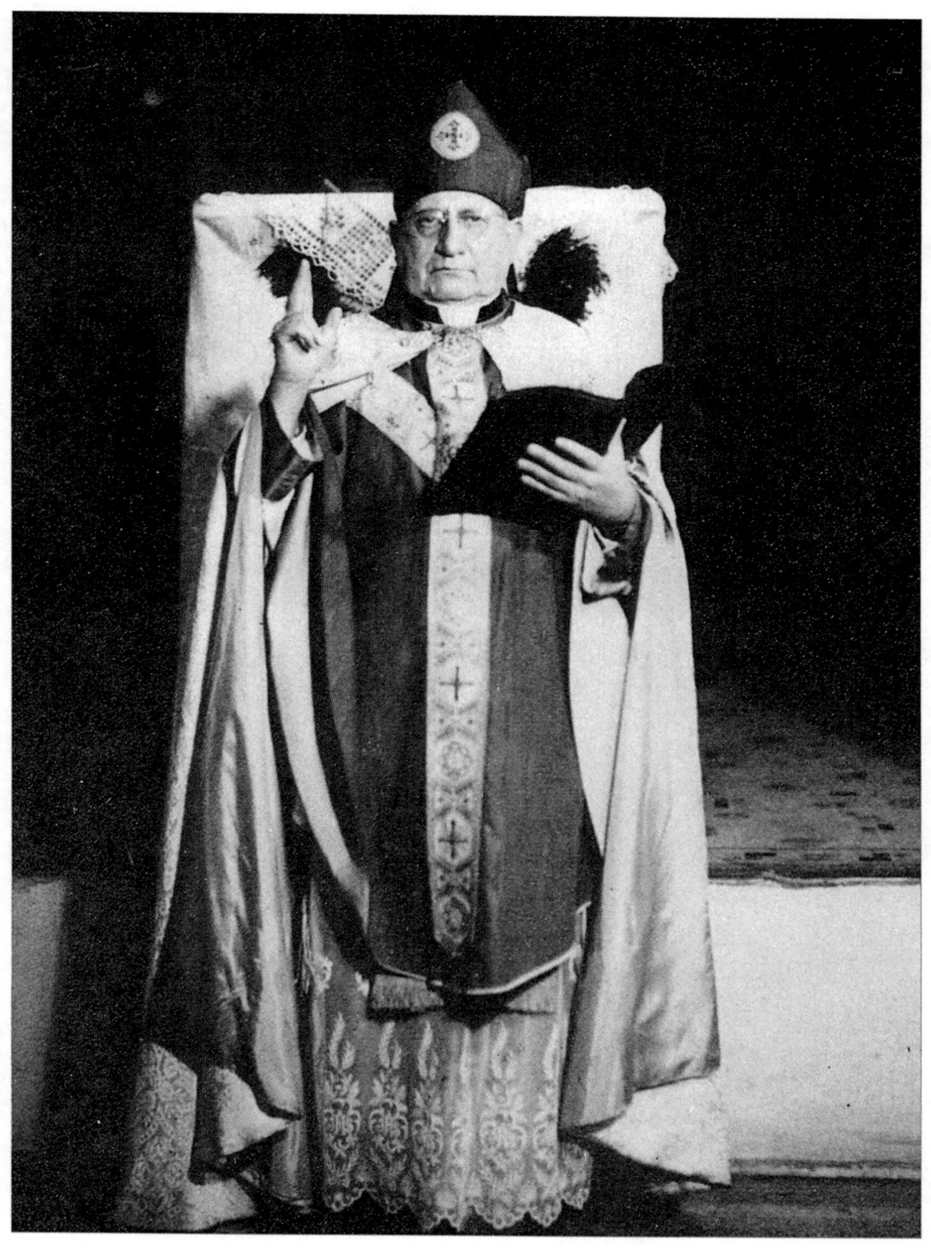

Roger's uncle Felix, an archbishop in the province of New Brunswick for the Roman Catholic Church.

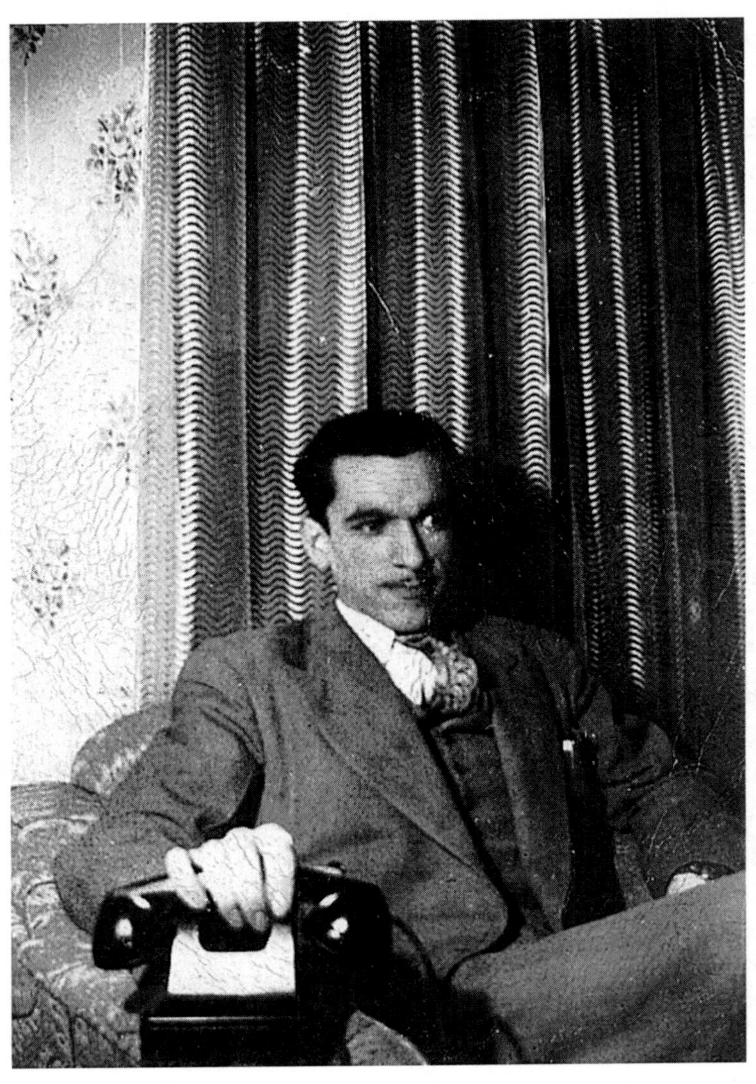

Roger at Cyril and Cynthia's home for his first Bible study—October 1946.
Roger was twenty-one years old.

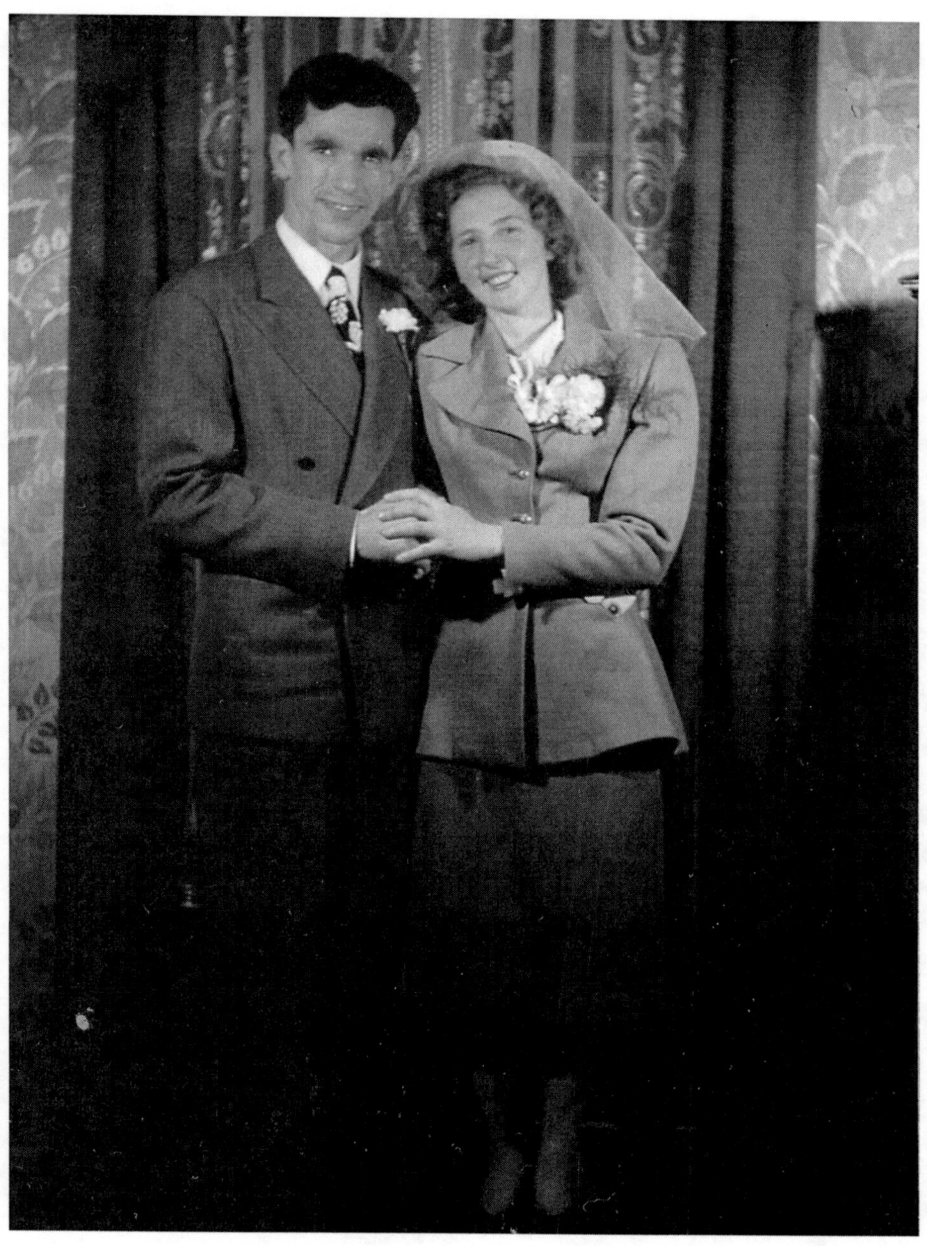

Roger and Hilda's wedding day in Montreal—September 1947.

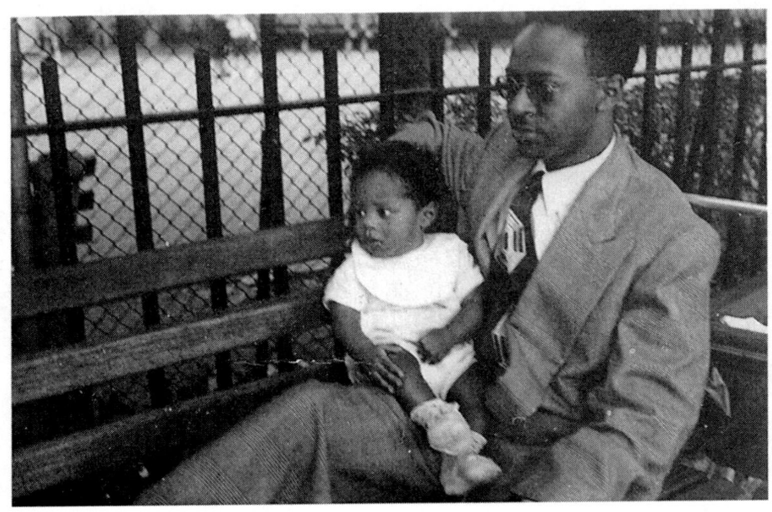

Cyril and Cynthia with Cyril Jr. in Montreal—1950.

Cyril and Cynthia going to church—1956.

Roger was a successful salesman for more than thirty years before becoming an author and starting an intercessory prayer ministry.

Cyril and Roger were lifelong friends. In the late 1970s, Cyril challenged Roger to write a book about his conversion story, and Cyril and Cynthia offered to type the manuscript. *A Trip Into the Supernatural* was released in 1982.

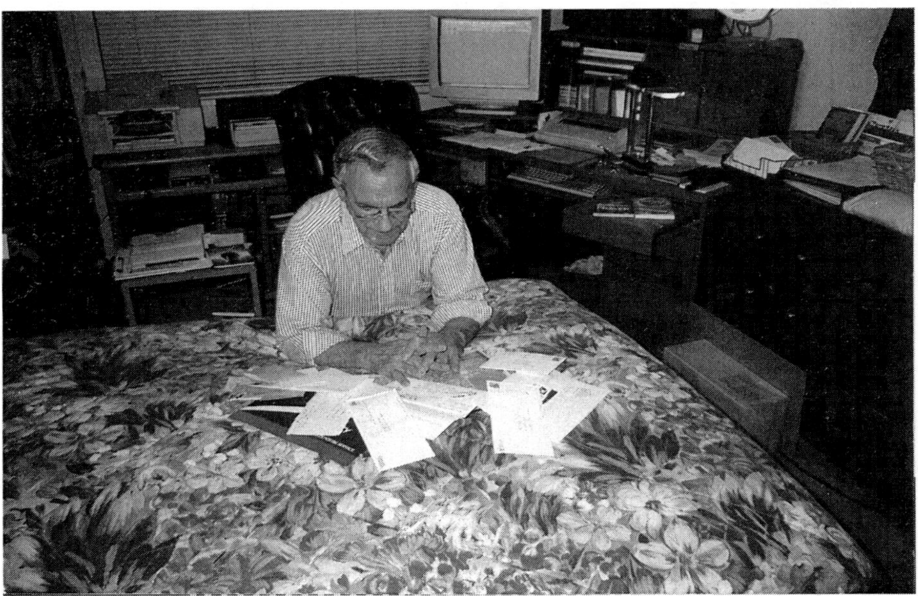

Roger kept several "prayer towers"—stacked bins with personal letters from all over the world. He often knelt by his bed to pray about them, which at the time of his death, numbered more than twenty thousand.

Roger and Hilda were married for more than fifty years. This picture was taken a few months before Roger's death in 1998.

Chapter 13

Evening at Study

Of the four Bible studies covered that Wednesday evening at Cyril's residence, one above all stands out in my mind. It was titled "The Destiny of the Wicked." By then, the Bible had revealed to me the Life-Giver as a God of love; a God who loved the world so much that He gave His only begotten Son that whosoever believes in Him, should not perish, but have everlasting life. And two additional declarations of Scripture reinforced this fact in my mind in a way that I will never forget.

First, that God sent not His Son into the world to condemn the world, but that the world through Him might be saved (John 3:17). Also, that God would have all men to be saved, and come unto the knowledge of the truth (1 Timothy 2:4). I had discovered that all of God's designs toward the descendants of Adam are prompted by love and grace.

I thought to myself, *How will such a God deal with those who do not choose to accept His way of life? Would such a decision on the part of those created at His hand cause this great Being to change from so noble a state of being to one who would be the direct opposite; that is, a God who takes pleasure in inflicting the cruelest of torture upon them for a duration of time never ending?* I was most anxious to find out what the Bible had to say about it.

Looking back on that study, we were first led to look into the origin of evil, its author, and how God will deal with that prince of angels when sin will have run its course. In Isaiah 14:12, we read, "How art thou fallen from heaven, O Lucifer, son of the morning!" In Ezekiel 28, and beginning with verse 12, we read of the high intellect possessed by Lucifer and the exalted position he occupied in the government of God. "Thus saith the Lord God; thou sealest up the sum, full of wisdom, and perfect in beauty. Thou hast been in Eden the garden of God; every precious stone was thy covering. . . . Thou art the anointed cherub that covereth; and I have set thee so. . . . Thou wast perfect in thy ways from the day that thou wast created, till iniquity was found in thee" (verses 12–15).

I was amazed at the account of the origin of evil given by the Word of God. How the mastermind Lucifer turned from admiring the beauty of God's character to self-admiration. Then that self-admiration turned into self-exaltation. "Thine heart was lifted up because of thy beauty, thou hast corrupted thy wisdom by reason of thy brightness" (verse 17). Lucifer's interest in self multiplied itself manyfold; and the time came when he had decided on a course of action that he felt could place him in equality with God in ruling part of the universe.

I enjoyed reading the account given by the prophet Isaiah: "For thou hast said in thine heart, I will ascend into heaven, I will exalt my throne above the stars of God: I will sit also upon the mount of the congregation, in the sides of the north: I will ascend above the heights of the clouds; I will be like the most High" (Isaiah 14:13, 14).

It was also very interesting to find out that there had been a war in heaven. Interesting as these accounts of Satan's rebellion were for me to read out of God's Holy Word, my greatest interest was to find out what God intended to do with the fallen cherub, after the time He has allocated him and his fallen angels to manifest their true character before the universe will have been completed.

Again, we read a declaration of God given to the prophet Ezekiel, "I will bring thee to ashes upon the earth in the sight of all them that behold thee. . . . Thou shalt be a terror, and never shalt thou be any more" (Ezekiel 28:18, 19). So it will be that the Life-Giver will bring the author of sin and death to an end. He will be brought to ashes upon the earth, and will no longer exist.

I thought to myself how final that declaration of God is. It leaves no place for misunderstanding. Its meaning cannot be understood to be anything but what the Bible says. When reading those words of Scripture for the first time, I thought to myself, and then said to Cyril and Cynthia, "How could some Christian theologians claiming to be authorities on the matters of religion and divinity preach that Satan will have eternal life in a lake of fire, when the Bible so plainly says the opposite?" Their reply was that my amazement over the clearness of the Bible on the subject had just begun.

And regarding Christian theologians and their having difficulties understanding the origin of evil, and the eternal destiny of the fallen cherub, and of those he has deceived, Cynthia went on to explain that one shouldn't be too surprised at that, when you think that one-third of the angels of heaven, beings of great intellect, became so confused over the issues involved in the great controversy between Christ and Satan that began in heaven, that in their confusion sided with Lucifer at the risk of eternal ruin. And keeping this thought in mind, one should not be surprised at the fact that large numbers of fallen mortals are confused and misunderstand the Word of God.

We then looked at what the Bible had to say concerning the eternal destiny of wicked human beings. In Psalm 37:20, we read that "the wicked shall perish, and the enemies of the LORD shall be as the fat of lambs: they shall consume; into smoke shall they consume away." This declaration of Scripture needed no explaining for me as to the extent of the destruction of those who will have rejected the mercies of God and persisted in ways of self-destruction.

My mind was carried back to the early thirties, when I was a little tyke. It was customary in those days for people living in the country to make their own laundry soap. At our place, my dad usually made soap during the cold winter months; it was more comfortable to do it that time, in that it required melting down large amounts of animal fat, and with additional ingredients combined with the above, boil the substance for many long hours over a huge stove in the barn.

With due respect to the hot stove, my brother Edgar and I were permitted to amuse ourselves by dropping bits of animal fat on the top of the roaring wood burning stove. We got great enjoyment at seeing how fast the substance would be consumed and vanish, never to be seen again. So the Bible made me aware that in like manner will be the eradication of evil doers and all traces of sin from the face of this planet, according to God's Holy Word.

After having read and considered a great many passages of Scripture on the subject, we closed the study by reading and reflecting on one major declaration of God, as to what the reward of the wicked will consist of. We read Malachi 4:1–3, "For, behold, the day cometh, that shall burn as an oven; and all the proud, yea, and all that do wickedly, shall be stubble: and the day that cometh shall burn them up, saith the LORD of hosts, that it shall leave them neither root nor branch. . . . And ye shall tread down the wicked; for they shall be ashes under the soles of your feet in the day that I shall do this, saith the LORD of hosts."

Cyril went on to explain that while the great Monarch of the universe is a God of love, at the same time He is a God of justice. While the element of love is the controlling power in His Being, we must never forget that those who reject His love and grace, His infinite sacrifice made through the death of His Son on Calvary, will have brought a condemnation upon themselves of the highest order; they will be guilty of rejecting the Spirit of grace.

"There will be a day," continued Cyril, "when God will execute the sentence of death that people will have brought upon themselves as we have seen in God's Holy Word. It will be eternal death, as spoken of by the apostle Paul: 'the wages of sin is death' " (Romans 6:23).

I then understood that the doctrine of eternal torment preached from Christian pulpits causes hundreds of thousands of people to put God away from their minds and their lives. Early in my life, I had fallen victim to its sophistry. I also realized that in order for anyone to study the destiny of the wicked from God's Holy Word, and get a correct understanding of it, one must understand that the law of love is the very foundation of the government of God; and that all of God's actions toward the people He has created are derived from that fountain of life and love, the heart of God. Keeping this in mind makes it impossible to believe in the doctrine of eternal torment.

This particular Bible study served to remove from my heart all that had embittered me toward God so early in my life, and had turned me into a God hater. As I said before, I saw justice and love walking hand in hand, and it was beautiful to behold. As we three conversed about the study just completed, Cyril went on to explain that the distresses of humanity that have taken place over the centuries are the direct result of Lucifer's action in heaven at the beginning of his great rebellion.

The high position he held in the government of God gave great power to what he said, giving substance to the claims he made. His real objectives were shrouded in mystery. The inhabitants of heaven couldn't visualize the end results of Lucifer's actions. Sin was a new element that was intruding its presence into every department of the Divine government. When Lucifer coveted the honor and power that was the prerogative of God alone to wield, he was violating the commandments of God.

The angels of heaven and the inhabitants of the galaxies were unable to comprehend the nature and the end result of sin. For the good of all, God had to allow a definite period of time to take place so that Lucifer and his associates, by their wicked deeds, would manifest the exceeding evil and malignity of sin. For some six thousand years, the inhabitants of the galaxies have been looking at the distresses of humanity with silent horror. An indelible impression has been made on their minds regarding the true nature of sin; and for this reason distress shall not rise a second time.

I was delighted over this description of the great conflict behind the scenes, as Cyril explained here, and I could have listened to him talk for hours, but he didn't want to give me spiritual indigestion (using his own words); he made one more statement before we turned our attention to something else.

"When all traces of sin shall have been wiped off the face of this little planet," he said, "and Christ will have re-created it in beauty superior to what it had been at its origin, then one pulse of harmony and happiness will beat throughout God's vast creation. What a wonderful age that will be."

The way Cyril and Cynthia opened before me the reality of the great spiritual conflict taking place between the forces of good and evil impressed me with the fact that the Holy Spirit of God was working, and had worked, in powerful and wonderful ways over the years, to bring me to the very place that I found myself that evening. I recall looking at my watch; the time was 9:20 P.M. I would have been conversing with demon worshipers had not the Spirit of God intervened in my life as He did. But here I was enjoying the blessed privilege of holding a Bible in my hands, God's Holy Word, and had by now definitely decided, with God's help, to break away from demon worship.

At every moment, the thought of it all caused a shiver to go up my spine; goose bumps caused the hair to stand up on my arms. I had experienced the equivalent of walking over Niagara Falls on a wire, and the Lord had brought me across safely. The reason prompting me to use this illustration is due to the fact that in 1954 when Hilda and I first came to the United States, we lived in Niagara Falls, New York, and almost every evening for about six months, we went to view the falls; Donald, our older son, was at that time five years old. It never failed that he had me tell him about the Frenchman Charles Blondin, who had walked over the the falls on a tightrope, pushing a wheelbarrow with his manager in it. We were all very impressed with the roaring Niagara, ever ready to swallow up the careless, and the story of the great feat accomplished by Blondin.

According to the legend, Blondin's manager had been making monetary arrangements regarding the great event. A town drunk had agreed to ride in the wheelbarrow for a reasonable sum of money (he would be sober at the time). All kinds of wagers had been placed on the feat, and for a whole month people on both sides of the Niagara hardly talked about anything else.

On the morning of the great event, the willing rider was nowhere to be found. Blondin's manager was unable to recruit a willing subject to take the ride. When he spoke about postponing the event till the next day, many of the thousands present threatened to throw him over the falls. The manager immediately calmed the people by announcing that he was going to be the passenger. He had ventured on a course of action that could very well have cost him his life, but there was no way out of it.

My spiritual experience in a way was very much like that of Blondin's manager. I had ventured on a course of action regarding spirit worship that seemed to offer me nothing but a life of well-being and fame. But in reality, I was about to plunge into the abyss of eternal ruin. At the conclusion of the study on the destiny of the wicked, I made mention to Cyril and Cynthia that during the days I had been memorizing Catholic catechisms, I had become acquainted with expressions and utterances derived from the Holy Scriptures to support the supposed never-ending punishments of the wicked. I could recall eternal fire, everlasting punishment, the smoke of their torment ascending forever and ever, and so forth.

My hosts both agreed that the Bible does carry such expressions, and that looking into the correct meaning of these constitutes a long study in itself, but a very worthwhile one that we should not neglect to have. It turned out that we had that interesting study three days later, conducted by Pastor L. W. Taylor, as I will recount later on.

As I retired that night, it was with the firm conviction that Cyril's God was indeed the Life-Giver, and the One to whom even demon spirits owed their existence. The fact that I had been able to study God's Holy Word without their interference testified to that. But on Thursday night, as I returned from Bible studies, I became aware that the spirits had visited my place. In like manner after my return home on Friday, I became very conscious that the spirits were trying to tell me something.

Chapter 14
The Bible Sabbath

I had promised my boss Harry that I would find out for him the reasons why Cyril observed the Bible Sabbath. In the interest of time, I will not cover the Bible studies we had had on Thursday and Friday, except the one on the seventh-day Sabbath. To begin with, Cyril explained that the Bible Sabbath, or the Lord's Day, is spoken of in the Holy Scriptures as being the seventh day of the week.

"In fact, in the fourth commandment of the Decalogue, written by God Himself, we are admonished to remember the Sabbath day to keep it holy," he said, then continued to explain. "The call to remember is probably due to the fact that humans are inclined in their busy daily activities to forget even some of the important things of life." We then turned to our Bibles and read the fourth commandment together. "Remember the sabbath day, to keep it holy. Six days shalt thou labour, and do all thy work: But the seventh day is the sabbath of the Lord thy God: in it thou shalt not do any work, thou, nor thy son, nor thy daughter, thy manservant, nor thy maidservant, nor thy cattle, nor thy stranger that is within thy gates: For in six days the Lord made heaven and earth, the sea, and all that in them is, and rested the seventh day: wherefore the Lord blessed the sabbath day, and hallowed it" (Exodus 20:8–11).

I was amazed to discover that the commandment of God, to keep the day He had blessed, was vastly different from the commandment I was instructed with from the Catholic catechism. In fact, I immediately told Cyril and Cynthia, "These are not the commandments of God that I memorized when I was a youngster."

I went to the first commandment and began to read, "I am the LORD thy God, which have brought thee out of the land of Egypt, out of the house of bondage. Thou shalt have no other gods before me. Thou shalt not make unto thee any graven image, or any likeness of any thing that is in heaven above, or that is in the earth beneath, or that is in the water under the earth. Thou shalt not bow down thyself to them, nor serve them: for I the LORD thy God am a jealous God" (Exodus 20:2–5).

In fact, I read all the commandments and found them to be greatly different in that these contained so much more detailed information. Then I found myself saying, "I have a hard time believing that these are the commandments of God." Cyril, using finesse and at the same time not minimizing the solemnity of the commandments, proceeded to say that indeed these were the commandments of God to the Hebrews as given to Moses. Then he made a statement in the form of a question that blew the issue wide open in my mind.

"Roger, I don't want to sound like I am a smart guy, but could it be that the commandments you were acquainted with were those of some other god?"

Then it dawned on me, as in my mind I visualized the so-called worship room of the gods, that the fallen cherubim, the demon god, had been at work in centuries past, tampering with God's holy commandments in order to mislead the human family. I understood why the Catholic Church's third commandment commands the faithful to sanctify Sunday as the Lord's Day. I then visualized the inhabitants of the whole earth being deceived by the master artist of deception.

I then said to my hosts, "Think of this, folks, the fallen Lucifer, the prince of this world, has the great religions of Buddhism, and of Islam, with its multimillions of followers, running after shadows. On the other hand, he has almost one billion Christians seeking a special blessing of the Creator on a day that He has neither blessed nor sanctified." Then I felt deeply in saying, "Pardon me, friends, but I feel I must give the devil the credit due him; truly, he is a clever demon and a hard worker."

The discovery I had just made was worth a lot to me, and had just triggered a new interest in my wanting to search out other avenues whereby the human family had been led away from their Creator. Returning to the study of the Bible Sabbath, I was impressed with the great emphasis placed by the Lord on the seventh day of the week as one to be remembered. We read, "And on the seventh day God ended his work which he had made; and he rested on the seventh day from all his work which he had made. And God blessed the seventh day, and sanctified it: because that in it he had rested from all his work which God created and made" (Genesis 2:2, 3).

One point that most vividly impressed my mind with the solemnity and sacredness placed upon that day by the Creator sank in when we considered that for forty years, the Lord fed the Israelites by raining bread from heaven on a daily basis except on the Sabbath day. We read the account, "Then said the LORD unto Moses, Behold, I will rain bread from heaven for you; and the people shall go out and gather a certain rate every day, that I may prove them, whether they will walk in my law, or no. And it shall come to pass, that on the sixth day they shall prepare that which they bring in; and it shall be twice as much as they gather daily" (Exodus 16:4, 5).

I found it interesting to see how the Lord sought to impress the Hebrews with the sacredness of His Sabbath. And as we read that account of the manna experience, I couldn't help but chuckle when I read that some of the folks back then, after all, were still wondering if God really meant what He said. Here it is, "Six days ye shall gather it; but on the seventh day, which is the sabbath, in it there shall be none. And it came to pass, that there went out some of the people on the seventh day for to gather, and they found none" (Exodus 16:26, 27).

Having taken into account the writings of Moses and the prophets on the matter of the Bible Sabbath, we turned to the New Testament to see how Jesus and the early disciples related to the Sabbath, and what their viewpoint was concerning it for the times ahead. We read about Jesus and His observance of the Sabbath in these words, "And he came to Nazareth, where he had been brought up: and, as his custom was, he went into the synagogue on the sabbath day" (Luke 4:16). Jesus declared to the Jewish people that He was the Lord of the Sabbath (Mark 2:28).

It was also very interesting for me to find that the Lord of the Sabbath never intended that His Father's holy law should ever be changed. For instance, we read an account that on one particular day, seeing the multitudes, He went up into a mountain and spoke to the people words of encouragement known to us today as the Sermon on the Mount; and in the very center of that sermon, our Lord made a statement that left no uncertainties in my mind regarding the solid foundation upon which God's holy law is established; and the Creator's determination that it should never be changed.

We read, "Think not that I am come to destroy the law, or the prophets: I am not come to destroy, but to fulfil. For verily I say unto you, Till heaven and earth pass, one jot or one tittle shall in no wise pass from the law, till all be fulfilled" (Matthew 5:17, 18). We also considered many biblical accounts of the early disciples and their observance of the Bible Sabbath.

After having read so much of the Word of God concerning the observance of the Creation Sabbath, I asked Cyril if he knew how Christians ever came to keep the first day of the week, or Sunday, as their day of rest. He went on to tell me that the Roman Catholic Church claims to have made the change in centuries past, by the power of God bestowed upon her.

"In fact," he said, "the church has no objections to letting people know that it has changed the commandments of God; and if you were to look into the church's writings, you could easily find an admission of it having accomplished that change."

At this time I wish to depart from the Bible study for a few minutes to tell you about my discovery on the above matter. On the following Sunday, I went to the municipal library in Montreal and did a little research in the religion department. Before long, I came across a Catholic catechism dating back to 1930 concerning the Sabbath of God, or what they classified as the third commandment. It gave very interesting information on how the Catholic Church brought about the change of its observance.

Six questions and answers explained it all.

Question: What is the third commandment?

Answer: The third commandment is: Remember that thou keep holy the Sabbath day.

Question: Which is the Sabbath day?

Answer: Saturday is the Sabbath day.

Question: Why do we observe Sunday instead of Saturday?

Answer: We observe Sunday instead of Saturday because the Catholic Church transferred the solemnity from Saturday to Sunday.

Question: Why did the Catholic Church substitute Sunday for Saturday?

Answer: The Church substituted Sunday for Saturday because Christ rose from the dead on a Sunday, and the Holy Ghost descended upon the apostles on a Sunday.

Question: By what authority did the church substitute Sunday for Saturday?

Answer: The church substituted Sunday for Saturday by the plenitude of that divine power which Jesus Christ bestowed upon her.

Question: What does the third commandment command?

Answer: The third commandment commands us to sanctify Sunday as the Lord's Day.

So, it was that in all honesty that the Roman Catholic Church admitted changing principles that are the very foundation of the Divine government, to soothe her whims and wishes. I was so impressed with my findings, that I committed the above to memory; which made a fine addition to my hobby of memorizing. And to add to my good fortune, in the early fifties I was able to acquire a copy of that very catechism, which I value highly.

Returning to the Bible study of the Sabbath of the Lord, to close the study we then looked into some of the benefits that the Lord has promised should bless the lives of those who by faith apply themselves to honor Him by obeying His requirement to keep holy His Sabbath day.

We turned to Isaiah 58, and Cynthia read verses 13 and 14 as Cyril and I followed along. I was deeply impressed with these words of the Lord; from the first time I heard them they caused me to desire that special blessing. But little did I realize then that the study on the Sabbath of the Lord covered on that particular evening in October 1946 would about twenty years later prove to be for me a most precious blessing. The Spirit of God blessed my mind, and those precious words were literally fulfilled when I was transported in my automobile that had run out of gas, when it was subzero temperature in the night, bringing me home safely, covering a distance of thirty-three miles.

It was in the early sixties, the exact year I cannot recall, but it was wintertime and we were living near Curriers, New York. On that particular evening, I had a business appointment set for 9:00 P.M. with a building contractor located southeast of Perry, New York. On the way to my destination, I realized that my gasoline was getting very low and at the same time it was getting close to my appointment time. I had taken a supposed shortcut to make better time, but in reality I had made a couple of bad turns and in so doing delayed my progress. Traveling rural roads was not what I was best at.

I stopped and obtained directions from some farm people on how to get to the gentleman's residence. As I traveled, I planned on getting gas after having completed my business transaction, as the service stations were then opened till 11:00 P.M., but things did not go exactly the way I had planned. Having arrived at the man's home, we became involved in talking business, and I forgot about time and gas.

When I left, it was 11:20 P.M.; the gentleman gave me some improved directions on how to get back home, and as I stepped out on the porch, I noticed the reading on the thermometer being at three degrees below zero. As I walked to my car, the snow creaked under my feet, indicating that the temperature would continue to drop.

The motor was slow to respond to the demands of the DieHard battery. With the noise of the heater blower going full force, and all my attention placed on the number of crossroads I had to pass before turning onto a main artery to familiar ground, I never noticed the gas gauge. Then all of a sudden, the motor began skipping; I took a look at the gas gauge, then terror struck my mind. The indicator was at its lowest reading.

To some people, to run out of gas in a rural area at that time of winter would perhaps not have alarmed them so much. But to me it was different; you see, when I was seventeen years of age, while spending a winter in Rouyn, Quebec, in northern Canada, I had the misfortune of freezing all my toes one morning when the temperature had dropped to forty below zero. I had to spend five months in a hospital, experiencing a series of skin grafts.

The day I was discharged from the hospital, my doctor asked me to listen attentively to him as he went about trying to impress my mind with the great danger facing me in the future. He stated that if ever I were to freeze my toes again, the only solution to the problem would then be amputation. So it was that terror that struck my mind when I realized that I was running out of gas. The last house I had passed must have been at least a couple of miles back. The car was slowing down, then picking up a little gas, would push ahead.

As I had done in other times of need, I raised my heart to Jesus for guidance. "Dear Jesus," I said, "give me help, lead me to do what is best for me in this emergency." Immediately, a great calm came over me. Then I thought to myself, *How mindless of me to worry about freezing my feet when for some twenty years I have been delighting myself in the observance of the Bible Sabbath. Now is the time for me to claim the promise of Isaiah 58:13, 14.*

My mind was carried back to that 1946 Bible study as if it had been yesterday, and I could hear Cynthia reading, "If thou turn away thy foot from the sabbath, from doing thy pleasure on my holy day; and call the sabbath a delight, the holy of the LORD, honourable; and shalt honour him, not doing thine own ways, nor finding thine own pleasure, nor speaking thine own words: then shalt thou delight thyself in the LORD; and I will cause thee to ride upon the high places of the earth, and feed thee with the heritage of Jacob thy father: for the mouth of the LORD hath spoken it."

The words of the Lord, "I will cause thee to ride upon the high places of the earth," stood before my mind in a special way. I thought, *There it is, the Life-Giver, the Author of all energy, told me years back that He would rejoice to propel me over Eagle Hill* [between Arcade and Eagle, New York], *and I sit here worrying; how foolish of me.*

Then in quick succession there passed before my mind Bible scenes of the ability of the God of the Bible Sabbath to handle emergencies. I visualized Hezekiah and the armies of Sennacherib, 185,000 men of war before Jerusalem ready to strike the blow of death, and how deliverance came. I thought of King Asa, being invaded by the multitudes of the Ethiopians and the Lubims, and the deliverance that came from the Lord.

You see, I had in times past memorized many of the great prayers of the Bible for encouragement. Now encouragement came, as the Spirit of God blessed my mind in a very special way. I visualized the Ancient of Days sitting on the eternal throne, the Author of all energy, with a fiery stream coming forth from before Him (energy in abundance); that great majesty with an entourage of a million persons in His magnificent temple.

I began to pray aloud; my conversation with the Lord went something like this, "My heavenly Father, thou great Monarch of the universe, Ancient of Days, thou God of the Bible Sabbath, I come before Thee as a most undeserving human being. I come for help, in the name of Christ Jesus, the Lord of glory who has accomplished an infinite sacrifice on Calvary, that it be possible for individuals such as myself, the most undeserving kind, to approach the throne of Thy divine majesty as I am doing at this moment." No sooner had I spoken those few words, and my car started to hum right up, accelerating to its previous speed. Then I realized that God was changing that most discouraging outlook for the glory of His own holy name.

I went on to tell my heavenly Father what a joy had been mine to serve Him since I had joined His commandment keepers; the people whom the spirits had declared to me that Satan hates. I thanked the Lord for the encouragement of His Holy Word as found in Chronicles, that "the eyes of the LORD run to and fro throughout the whole earth, to shew himself strong in the behalf of them whose heart is perfect toward him" (2 Chronicles 16:9). I told the Lord that while I myself was lacking in many ways in Christian virtues, my Redeemer is perfect in all points, and that I trusted in the merits of His great righteousness to carry me on in my pilgrimage through the land of the enemy.

My conversation with the Lord, and my quoting Bible passages as the Spirit of God brought them to my remembrance, continued for about forty-five minutes; and that car of mine never slowed down, but up and over the hills it went. My heart began to beat rapidly when I turned into our driveway and realized that my automobile had been energized by the element of creation, the type used by God during the Creation week. As I arrived at our side entrance, the motor stopped; I turned the ignition off, ran into the house, woke up my wife, and told her about my deliverance by the power of God. We had a session of thanksgiving and then retired for the night.

Returning to the study of the Bible Sabbath, I must say that while my first interest was to bring back to my Jewish boss an explanation of Cyril's religious convictions on the matter, my next one was to find out how and where Christians became so involved with Sunday; or in other words, involved with the day of the sun, that I researched in the months ahead and made some most interesting discoveries.

In addition to my boss's interest in Cyril's Sabbath, and my newly created inquisitiveness, someone else's interest became aroused in the subject also—demon spirits. I will explain a little further on how the evening of the coming Saturday on my return home, they went on to reestablish contact with me; and about their hatred of the Bible Sabbath.

On that Friday evening, at the conclusion of the Sabbath study, Cyril and Cynthia invited me to attend church with them the next day. Cyril explained that on that Sabbath he would be baptized by immersion, and become a member of the Seventh-day Adventist Church. I was pleased with the invitation and expressed my interest to be with them for that occasion. It was agreed that I would come to their residence and from there we would proceed to church.

Chapter 15

A New Day and a New Life

Sabbath morning I arrived at the Grossés' residence and found that a couple of friends had come to join them at church. We were introduced, chatted a bit, and as my custom was, I pulled out my cigarettes and offered them one, but they politely declined. Then the thought entered my mind that it could very well be that Adventists abstain from smoking, it being a church ordinance. A short while later, as we were walking out of the house, I asked Cyril about it. He then informed me that Adventists are very health conscious, not as a means of obtaining favor with God, but in the interest of good health; seeing that healthy people enjoy more of the fullness of life. At the same time, he also mentioned that one of the Bible studies soon to be covered pertained to healthful living, and that the benefits to be derived by abstaining from using tobacco would then be presented.

I immediately assured him that I would abstain from smoking while in the presence of church members that day. Then I thought to myself, *How in the world am I going to do it?* At the same time, I said to myself, *How fortunate I am that these young people didn't tell me at the beginning of the Bible studies that I shouldn't smoke; my addiction would surely have caused me to refuse studying with them.*

At a later date, as I was conversing with Cyril about the fact that tobacco had had such a hold on my life, and that I would undoubtedly have refused to study with them had they made reference to my smoking, he informed me that after presenting the matter before the Lord, they had been impressed to put up with it in order to first acquaint me with Christ. I was not aware at the time that Cyril and Cynthia were deeply involved in a ministry of reconciliation. Their main objective was to reconcile Roger Morneau to the Life-Giver. And in this involvement they were being led by the Spirit of God.

For instance, when I told Cyril that morning that I would not smoke in the presence of church people, he rejoiced that their prayers were being answered, as he told me later. You see, before inviting me to go to church with them, they had asked the Lord to bless my life in a special way. They asked for two miracles to take place.

First, they asked that I should be made to see and appreciate the sacredness of the Bible Sabbath. This having taken place, they would ask me to go to church with them; and if I accepted their invitation, it would be a sign that God was working a miracle of redemption. And second, they prayed that God would take away from me the craving for tobacco, so I would not be tortured by a craving for the weed.

How wonderfully their prayers were answered. The thought of tobacco never entered my mind until about 7:00 P.M. that evening. Then for two hours my body went through an agony such as I had never experienced, leading me to conclude that I was in great need of a Savior. One who could perform a miracle of love by removing lord Nicotine, who had enthroned himself in every fiber of my body. That miracle of love was performed late that evening, as I will recount shortly.

It was a beautiful day, that Sabbath morning of October 1946 in Montreal, Canada. Walking to church was indeed preferable to taking the tramways, in that nature was beautifully alive, the air was crisp, and bright rays of sunshine pierced through the trees and showered the earth with a thousand kisses of love. The city birds seemed to be happier that day, and everything around us told of a God of love watching over all.

Having fresh in my mind verses of Scripture concerning the Sabbath of Creation, the day carried a new meaning for me. Saturday would never be quite the same as it had been in the past. I was now an informed individual regarding planet Earth and its relation to the rest of the universe, as well as the demands placed upon its inhabitants by the Creator. Saturday would be from then on the Sabbath day, a day to remember.

So we proceeded to church; I a spiritualist, walking with Sabbath keepers to an Adventist church. These friends were not yet aware of the fact that I was slowly stepping out of the ranks of the fallen Lucifer, their most vicious enemy. It had been but a few days since I had had my last contact with demon spirits.

As we approached the church, I was surprised to see that almost every person on the sidewalk was turning to the church and making their way into the sanctuary. Coming near the entrance, we merged with others entering. We were pleasantly welcomed to Sabbath School and given a church bulletin. Nearby, I noticed a rack containing church literature, periodicals, and tracts. I reached over and picked up a brochure. Once in the sanctuary, I was impressed by a well-attended church.

After seating ourselves, I began to read that attention-getting tract, while sacred music was being played softly. The tract gave detailed information concerning the church's organizations and various fields of activities. The number of schools operated by the denomination amounted to thousands; plus its academies, colleges, and universities were then numbered in the hundreds.

Its mission work was carried into more than one hundred countries. Its medical ministry impressed me highly in that its sanitariums and hospitals were well over a hundred, and in addition to that, dispensaries and clinics amounted into the hundreds. Its disaster preparedness was very impressive to read about. It told of medical aid centers scattered around the world, stocked with food, blankets, clothing, and other supplies ready to distribute to areas hit by natural or man-made disasters.

I saw that the Spirit of God was blessing the minds of its people with an understanding of the true values of life; causing them to carry forward the great plan of mercy and benevolence of the Lord Jesus, in feeding the hungry, clothing the naked, and preaching the gospel of a soon-returning Savior to a perishing world.

A genuine friendly welcome was given to all, and the Sabbath School service began. The period leading to the study of God's Word was indeed interesting, inspiring, and informative to a person visiting an Adventist church for the first time. I saw a people dedicated to being a blessing to their fellow humans.

A period of about forty minutes was devoted to Bible study. The visitors' class was taught by Pastor L. W. Taylor. The lesson of the day was on the life of Christ. The central theme being that Jesus of Nazareth, while on earth, ruled His life by the principles of the Word of God, leaving us an example to follow.

Pastor Taylor made a statement that I have retained to this day and will never forget. He said that "if we follow our Lord's example, there will come to us peace, contentment, and wisdom that the world can neither give or take away." Those words could not have come at a better time. The many studies of the Word of God covered in a few days, culminating in that of the Bible Sabbath, had led me to desire to turn my life over to the Lord Jesus, with the decision to observe the seventh-day Sabbath. Pastor Taylor's statement was indeed a motivating factor in my becoming a commandment keeper.

I found the Sabbath School Bible study period very interesting and wished that it had lasted longer. The eleven o'clock worship hour was also very inspiring, and culminated in a baptismal service, of which one of the candidates was my newfound friend, Cyril. When Cyril was back at my side, I stated that, God willing, I would be there again on the coming Sabbath. I also indicated the interest of conversing with Pastor Taylor, when the occasion would present itself, regarding eternal realities.

On our way out of the sanctuary, Cyril asked the pastor if it be possible for him to give us some of his time that afternoon, explaining that I would be spending the day at their home. The minister was very kind, and offered to pay us a visit instead of us coming to his parsonage office. As we walked out of the church, I couldn't help but thank Cyril and Cynthia for their interest in my well-being. At that moment, it was not possible for them to understand exactly the extent of the blessings they had brought to my life. The Spirit of God had made them instrumental in bringing me to a spiritual oasis, where I could be regenerated by Christ, the Lord of glory, who had spoken into existence all the autumn beauty that I had beheld in the changing leaves of that beautiful October day.

That memorable Sabbath day was laced with a series of *firsts:* For instance, it was the first time I observed the Bible Sabbath. It was my first time entering a Seventh-day Adventist church. It was also the first time I had read anything about the medical missionary work carried on by the Adventist Church. It was my first time at witnessing a baptism by immersion. And last but not least, I ate my first vegetarian meal. As we arrived at the Grossés' residence, it was but a few minutes until Cynthia served us a magnificent vegetarian meal. It had been prepared the day before and only needed reheating to make it not only appealing to the eye, but most palatable and nourishing. I almost forgot, in addition to this, I must say that it was also my first time at having a six-hour Bible study with a minister.

At about two thirty that afternoon, Pastor Taylor arrived and after visiting for a while, the conversation turned to religious matters. I mentioned that we had been studying the Bible during the past week and I had become acquainted with wonderful truths about eternal realities. He inquired as to how much studying we had done, and what subjects had been the object of our attention.

I enumerated some of the topics covered, mentioning that we had had over twenty Bible studies. I remember that moment as if it were yesterday. Pastor Taylor's eyes opened wide with amazement, then he asked if he had heard correctly, stating the amount. When assured that what he had heard was right, he said, "Do you mind telling me what brought about this diligent study?"

I can't recall exactly the reason given, but I'd like to expand a little on this by saying that in turn I was surprised to see that the good pastor was a little shocked over the number of Bible studies we had had. I thought that anyone coming across Bible truth as I had would study the Scriptures in like manner, using the same diligence in acquiring spiritual knowledge. Before leaving for home that evening, Cyril and Cynthia told me something interesting, and that cleared things up for me.

Some time back, many of the church members were interested in knowing how to share their religious convictions with people not of their faith who asked them for a reason for the hope they held dear to themselves. They asked their minister if he would be kind enough to conduct some classes that would make it interesting and at the same time beneficial to the inquirer.

So it was that Pastor Taylor counseled them in using moderation in studying the Good Book with those who had not previously been acquainted with the Word of God. He had stated that to hold Bible studies once or twice a week should be the ideal, in that it gave a person time to understand and appreciate those great truths of the Word of God, which have long been lost sight of by the Christian world.

The pastor was right in suggesting moderation to his church members in their Bible study activities. In my case, it was an exception, and the Spirit of God blessed Cyril's and Cynthia's minds, leading them to do what was right for me. Time was not mine to use in a leisurely manner.

Now, returning to that pastoral visit, I mentioned to Pastor Taylor the deep impressions made upon my mind while attending the Sabbath services of his church that morning. I continued conversing with him and inquired why other Protestant churches were not observing the Bible Sabbath of Creation, when God had prescribed its observance as a means of obtaining a very special blessing; one He has never placed on any other day of the week.

Pastor Taylor went on to answer my inquiry by first stating that the Seventh-day Adventist Church is in reality a church of prophecy. As John the Baptist was raised of God to proclaim to the people of his day who had lost sight of the Messianic prophecies that the Redeemer of humanity was among them, so God has raised the Adventist Church to be a voice crying out in the wilderness of these modern days, "Prepare ye the way of the Lord."

Regarding the many Protestant churches not observing the Bible Sabbath, he explained how God does not urge His ways upon people; on the contrary, He desires from all a service of love; homage that springs from an intelligent appreciation of His divine character. He takes no pleasure in a forced allegiance, and for those reasons He grants a freedom of choice to all that they may render Him voluntary service.

After conversing a bit more, I realized that in no way could I keep to myself the secret that was mine, concerning my experience with spirit worship. My deep interest in religious matters made it obvious to Pastor Taylor that some powerful motivating factor was involved. As reluctant as I was to talk about my affiliation with demon spirits, I felt that having decided to break away from that evil power, the pastor could give me guidance that could prove most valuable to me in the struggle that I was sure to encounter; knowing that demon spirits do not give up easily.

Once my activities as a spiritist were disclosed, Pastor Taylor directed my attention to the Source of all life and power, Christ Jesus. He stated that "in him dwelleth all the fulness of the Godhead bodily. And ye are complete in him, which is the head of all principality and power" (Colossians 2:9, 10).

The revelation that all principalities and powers, including that the fallen cherub and his associates owe their very existence to Christ, the Lord of glory, was very encouraging to me and proved to be a real blessing that very night during an encounter with the spirits. Additional verses of Scripture were brought forth by the pastor that served to establish in my mind the superior power of our great Redeemer, versus that of the fallen Lucifer and his demon spirits.

What we had conversed about up to then had been very interesting and enlightening to me, but now I was looking for an opening to engage the good pastor in explaining some of the biblical expressions used by the proponents of the immortality of man. I didn't have to wait very long before he asked me if there were any additional questions in my mind that needed some clarification. Without hesitation, I stated that there were. I briefly touched on a few of the discoveries I had made from the Word of God that week, leading to a major question for him to resolve.

I mentioned that our studying of God's Holy Word that week had revealed to me that humans are completely mortal, contrary to the popular belief held through most of Christendom that when a person dies he or she does not completely die, but has a supposedly immortal soul that proceeds to one's reward or scene of punishment.

I continued, "The Bible declares that God alone has immortality, or in other words, man is fully mortal. We have read many biblical passages setting forth the fact that immortality will be given to the redeemed of the Lord at the resurrection that takes place at the second coming of Christ.

"We have been made aware of the fact that the unrighteous, not having immortality, will cease to exist once the punishment inflicted upon them has been carried out. But notwithstanding the fact that the Word of God is so precise, so clear on declaring that the ungodly will cease to exist, there are passages of Scripture that seem to indicate the opposite.

"As a youngster memorizing Catholic catechisms, I became acquainted with expressions derived from the Holy Scriptures to support the supposed never-ending punishment of the wicked. I can recall: eternal fire, everlasting punishment, the smoke of their torment shall ascend forever and ever, and so forth. So, Pastor Taylor, I would appreciate very much if you could clarify for me what seems to be a contradiction in the Word of God."

A sense of deep satisfaction came over me as he stated that there was no contradiction in the Word of God, but a lack of understanding on the part of those who cherish the doctrine of the immortal soul.

Pastor Taylor went on to explain that many people misunderstand the meaning of the word *punishment.* They define the word *punishment* as a conscious suffering, and believe that when any affliction is no longer realized by the senses, it ceases to be a punishment. But as we look into human penalties, we find that a punishment is estimated by the loss involved and not merely by the amount of pain inflicted.

He continued, "For instance, why is the sentence of death recognized as the greatest punishment? It is not because the pain involved is greater, because some minor forms of torture, such as whipping, inflict more pain upon the offender than decapitation or hanging. But death is recognized as the greatest because it is the most lasting. It deprives its victim permanently of all the relations and blessings of life; and its length is estimated by the life the person would have enjoyed if it hadn't been inflicted. So it is," he said, "when death is inflicted from which there is to be no release, that is to say no resurrection, that punishment is everlasting, or eternal. By the terrible infliction of the second death, the sinner will be deprived of the bright and ceaseless years of eternal or everlasting life. And because that life is everlasting, the loss or the punishment is everlasting also."

What a logical approach to solving what appeared to be a Bible contradiction of the highest magnitude!

"Pastor," I said, "I like your sensible way of treating this particular subject. I don't wish to impose upon your kindness, but would you please tell me more regarding this subject?"

He continued by saying, "In Bible language, the word *everlasting* and the word *eternal,* because they are associated with other words such as the *fire* and *punishment,* simply denote the results produced by the fire or the punishment; and not the continuation of the process of burning and punishing."

What a statement, I thought; *I hope he has biblical passages to back that up.* I was all ears; I sat on the edge of my chair. I was getting excited as the pastor was about to reduce another one of my childhood mysteries to vapor.

"Anything wrong?" asked the pastor.

"No, sir, not at all, I am just adjusting my sitting position a little; please continue."

"I'd like to give you three short examples," said the pastor. "In Hebrews 5:9, we read of *eternal salvation,* which is a salvation that is eternal or everlasting in its results; not a salvation that is forever going on but never accomplished. In Hebrews 6:2, the apostle Paul speaks of *eternal redemption.* Not a redemption through which we are eternally approaching a redeemed state that we never reach, but a redemption that releases us for all eternity from the power of sin and death."

The pastor went on a little further by saying that when the Bible speaks of eternal fire, it is making reference to a fire that produces results that are eternal or everlasting. "We are told in Jude 7," he said, "that the cities of Sodom and Gomorrah are set forth as an example of the suffering of the vengeance of eternal fire. The apostle Peter, speaking on the same subject, tells us that God turned the cities of Sodom and Gomorrah into ashes, making them an example 'unto those that after should live ungodly' " (2 Peter 2:6).

My mind was delighted at the way the Bible explained itself. I had never heard anyone speaking so fluently and knowledgeably on the subject. Every word the pastor spoke was backed up by sound biblical references and left no doubt of the goodness and love of God for those created in His image.

However, there remained in the back of my mind one expression deeply rooted; planted by the religious instruction received when I was a youngster and intended by proponents of the doctrine of the immortal soul, that it should never be uprooted for the rest of life. For a moment, I felt reluctance in bringing it forth; I felt that in no way could the good pastor have an explanation of the term. Then I thought that if he came forth with a down-to-earth explanation, as he did for the other biblical expressions we had covered, what a marvelous thing it would be; it would for all times establish in my mind the fact that the God of the Bible is, in the fullest sense of the word, a God of *love*.

I proceeded in this manner, "Pastor Taylor, I must admit that the way you have been conversing regarding spiritual matters has impressed me deeply with the fact that you have been an avid student of the Word of God; and I admire the wisdom with which you speak concerning matters of eternal importance. Again, I don't wish to impose on your kindness, but I would appreciate very much if you would clarify for me one last biblical expression."

"Well, I am glad to hear that I have been of some help to you, what else would you like to know?"

"Pastor, what do you get from this expression of the Holy Scriptures: 'the smoke of their torment shall ascend forever and ever'?" I sat back in the solid comfort of that overstuffed living room chair and anxiously waited for the pastor's reply.

With an air of confidence that can be conveyed only by a person of experience in dealing with difficult subjects, Pastor Taylor proceeded to answer my inquiry. He explained that in the Holy Scriptures the phrase *forever and ever* is applied to things that endure for a long time, or an indefinite period of time. It is applied to the Jewish priesthood, to the Mosaic ordinances, to the possession of the land of Canaan, to the hills and mountains, to the earth, to the time of service to be rendered by a slave, and so forth.

He continued, "The phrase denotes a duration or continuation of time, the length of that duration being determined by the nature of the objects to which it is applied. When applied to things that we know from other declarations of the Scriptures are to have no end, it signifies an eternity of being; but when applied to things that are to end, it is correspondingly limited in its meaning."

Honestly, I was astonished at the expertise manifested in the way the pastor approached the subject, and what he said made a lot of sense. He went on to clarify his statements by using a few verses of Scripture. "In Exodus 21:2–6, we read that during the Mosaic dispensation, if a Hebrew bought a servant, in the seventh year the servant could go free. But in the case where a servant didn't wish to leave the service of his master, that servant could relinquish his rights to freedom by following some specific instructions. The master would bring his servant to the judges and in their presence would have the servant stand by a door post. Then he would bore his ear through with an awl, and his servant would then serve him forever. In this case, the term *forever* could mean duration of time anywhere from one day to many years, depending on how long the servant would live."

Pastor Taylor continued by saying that another interesting use of the term *forever* is found in Psalm 21:1, 4. King David was very appreciative and thankful to God for the many times his life had been spared. And in the verses just mentioned, he tells the Lord, "The king shall joy in thy strength, O LORD; and in thy salvation how greatly shall he rejoice! . . . He asked life of thee, and thou gavest it him, even length of days for ever and ever." David lived to be quite old, so the phrase *forever and ever* in this instance probably represented a duration of time consisting of many years.

Having set forth biblical examples showing how limited the term *forever and ever* can be, when applied to things that are to end, Pastor Taylor then used a Bible reference where the phrase *forever and ever* signifies an eternity of being. We turned to Daniel 2, and considered Daniel's interpretation of King Nebuchadnezzar's dream of the great image. How the various metals making up that great image represented great kingdoms that were to take place in times to come. And in verse 44, we read that "in the days of these kings shall the God of heaven set up a kingdom, which shall never be destroyed . . . and it shall stand for ever." We found also, in chapter 7 that the saints of the Most High will possess the kingdom "for ever, even for ever and ever" (verse 18).

Pastor Taylor, having made sure that I saw things as they truly are in the light of the Bible, went on to say that just as we are plainly assured in the Holy Scriptures that Christ's kingdom, once established upon earth, will be an everlasting kingdom, and that the existence of the righteous will be eternal, or never ending, in like manner we are instructed in the Good Book that the existence of the wicked will cease in the second death, which will take place in the lake of fire (Revelation 21:8).

What a glorious experience that Bible study had been for me. In reality, I saw a mountain of darkness and error roll away and vanish. So-called mysteries that had perplexed the minds of my Catholic parents in their efforts to associate the character of a God of love with the doctrine of eternal torment had melted away, as would a gigantic iceberg under a tropical sun. Another benefit I had gained was the assurance that the Word of God doesn't contradict itself.

So it was that on that beautiful Sabbath day of October 1946, the righteousness of the Son of God shone upon me from the Holy of Holies of God's heavenly sanctuary; the Spirit of God blessed the minds of His servants, causing them to minister to my great needs in a manner that only divine wisdom knew how.

Chapter 16
A Miracle of Love

The entire day had been taken up with factors of great interest to me, serving to enlarge my understanding of God's great love for the fallen human family. It was about 7:00 P.M. when all of a sudden a deep craving for a cigarette took place. To my amazement, I realized that I hadn't smoked all day, and hadn't even thought of it. Then I figured that my mind had been so taken up with matters of higher interest, that it had produced a forgetfulness of the weed. In the light of that reasoning, I concluded that I could put tobacco from my mind and my lungs if I kept occupied with good things.

So our conversation on spiritual things continued, with my bringing forth questions to Pastor Taylor that had perplexed my mind in times past. I was in reality very impressed that the pastor had a "Thus saith the Lord" for every human inquiry.

Then I began to experience a real problem. I was craving for a cigarette in a bad way. The saliva in my mouth was thickening, to the point that it became difficult for me to talk. My nostrils began to burn in the manner usually experienced when coming down with a cold. After a while, I became restless, changing my sitting position often, seeking to find a relaxing one. I developed a headache, something I seldom had; it ached all the way down the back of my neck.

At my insistence, Pastor Taylor conversed with us on the subject of religion till about 9:00 P.M. After his departure, the first thing I did was light a cigarette, and continued smoking nonstop for about an hour. To my great surprise, all my physical distresses went away.

Cyril and Cynthia covered with me the Bible study on healthful living, comprising the subject of tobacco. It was very informative and served to make me aware that I was enslaved by a health-destroying habit. I, there and then, determined to give it up; realizing that I would have to go through an awful struggle to do it—unless Cyril's God, the Lord of the Sabbath, the One who had stilled the Sea of Galilee, He who had blessed my life that very day by giving me deliverance from the power of the weed for so many hours, would be willing to deliver me from it on a permanent basis.

A short while later, I thanked my friends for their kindness toward me and the very meaningful day they had made possible, and left for home. On the tramway, I kept reviewing in my mind the events of the day, and especially my episode with tobacco, realizing that I had more than one powerful enemy. During the travel time, I came up with a plan of action that I was sure would put an end to the tobacco problem.

Pastor Taylor had made me aware of the great redeeming power there is in the merits of the precious blood of Christ, the Lord of glory, shed on Calvary. In fact, he led me to see and understand that the fallen cherub and his associates, the fallen angels, can be overcome only through the power we read about in Revelation 12:11, "And they overcame him by the blood of the Lamb."

I arrived home that evening at about 11:30 P.M. On my door was a note to call my friend Roland at his residence, regardless of how late it was. I said to myself, *This will have to wait a while.* As I entered the place, I noticed that the spirits had been restless; most everything was out of place. I was not troubled over that, because I had become accustomed to dealing with the unusual.

I took three cartons of cigarettes I had in my closet and placed them on a table. I then took my Bible and opened it to Matthew 27, and read from verse 24 to 54 about the crucifixion of the Lord of glory. Then, placing the open Bible on the cartons of cigarettes, I knelt by the table and raised my heart to the Holy of Holies of the heavenly sanctuary and began to converse with my great High Priest about my problems. I told the Lord Jesus about His amazing love for the undeserving. I thanked Him for blessing my life, even when I was an open enemy of His, blaspheming His name. I confessed my sins and acknowledged the evil of my heart.

Pastor Taylor had made me aware of the fact that Christ Jesus' ministry in the heavenly sanctuary is taking place to help people in trouble and that He specializes in hopeless cases. Those words of the pastor had kindled great hope in my heart, causing me to think that if Jesus specializes in hopeless cases, here was a real hopeless case for Him to work on. With the troubles I had, I was facing encounters with enemies far too clever and powerful for me.

I thanked the Lord for encouraging my heart toward Him and His Holy Word. I acknowledged the fact that demon spirits had been held back from me, by the power of His love. And because of this, I wanted to turn my life over to

Him, to serve Him as He saw fit. I told Jesus that I was a hopeless case, and seeing that He specialized in hopeless cases, I was willing to turn over to Him my body and my mind for Him to re-create. And this being done, I would then delight myself in the Lord by remembering His Sabbath day to keep it holy. Pointing to the cartons of cigarettes, I said, "Lord Jesus, please deliver me from this powerful enemy, break the power it has upon me as You have manifested Your ability to do so this day. Remove that insatiable desire for the weed. In fact, Lord, remove from my body the very element of death."

I talked with the Lord for some time, because my needs for His grace were many. I thanked Him for having heard me and for blessing my life. I then rose from my knees, took the cigarettes to the bathroom, opened every package, tore them up, and flushed them down the toilet. For Roger Morneau, it was the end of smoking. From that time on, I never touched a cigarette, and never had the desire to do so. In a wonderful way, the Lord Jesus had performed a miracle of love.

After my conversation with the Lord Jesus in prayer over my problem, and disposing of my three cartons of cigarettes, I sat in my rocker and picked up a book to read. As I did, the piece of paper with the message on it to phone Roland began to levitate and float around the room, then it was slapped on my open book with such force that it knocked the book out of my hands and almost off my lap. My first impulse was to tell the spirit a thing or two, but I had determined that regardless what would take place in their activities, I would not get involved in verbal communication with them. I took the piece of paper and placed it between pages of the book and continued to read. A short while later, the book was pulled out of my hands and thrown against the wall on the opposite side of the room.

Not because of the pressure applied by the spirit, but due to respect for my friend, I decided to go and phone him. There was a pay phone in the hallway, but in this case, I would not use it, so I went to a restaurant down the street. As I sat in the phone booth, I looked at my watch; it was 1:00 A.M. The phone rang twice.

"Hello! Morneau, is this you?"

"Yes, it is."

"Morneau, you daredevil! What am I saying; I didn't mean it that way. I meant to say that you are gambling with your life; have you lost your mind?"

My reply was, "You sound so upset, friend, what is your problem?"

"My problem, I have no problem; you are the one in great trouble and you sound as if you haven't got a care in the world. Morneau, I have always admired your daring spirit, but now you have gone too far; you have gone way too far. You have turned against yourself the power of the spirits that have benefited you, and you are going to be destroyed. I am surprised at the fact that you are still alive. I am concerned over you, man; it's because I care for your well-being that I have been sitting by this phone all evening waiting for your call. Don't you have anything to say?" my friend responded.

"Of course I have something to say, but how can I say anything when you have not given me a chance to talk?" I replied.

Without waiting even a moment, he went on talking again. He was very upset. "Morneau, you don't understand the extent of the trouble you are in. By Wednesday evening, according to the satanic priest, you were in deep trouble with the spirits. But now, it is too late, too late."

"Roland, if you calm down and take hold of yourself, it would be much easier for us to understand one another. Now, explain yourself about Wednesday evening and this 'now being too late.' "

He then regained his composure to the point that the tone of his voice abated to its normal range. "Last Wednesday when I entered our place of worship, I was whisked into the high priest's office. He asked if I had seen you in the past week. His facial expressions led me to understand that something awful had happened. I asked if you were dead, maybe you had an accident. He stated that you were in a situation more horrible than that. On Tuesday night, during the sacred hour of midnight [the hours of noon and midnight are sacred, according to demon spirits], a spirit counselor appeared to him and told of your being involved in studying the Bible with Sabbath keepers; the very people the master hates most on the face of the earth. I was asked to try to get a hold of you and make you aware of the danger you are in, but I couldn't reach you."

"Roland, I'd like you to know first that everything is under control; I am in no great danger."

"That's what you think. At six thirty this evening, the high priest called to inform me that according to the spirits, you have been in church today with those Sabbath people, and that has infuriated the master to the highest degree. What do you have to say about that?"

"Yes, I have been studying the Bible, and have gone to a Bible Sabbath-keeping church; and I couldn't care less about the way the fallen cherubim feel about me. If you like to know more about my activities of the past week, why don't you come over to see me in the morning and I will tell you all about it?"

We agreed on 10:00 A.M. and ended the conversation. On my return home, I prayed to the Lord Jesus and then went to bed. I must have been in bed about twenty minutes when the lights went on. I turned them off and went back to bed. Almost instantly, they were back on again. I then decided to sleep with the lights on. A couple of minutes later, almost everything was being moved out of place. A picture on a wall would move across the room and hang on the opposite wall. A table lamp moved from its place, and hung in midair without any visible support. As I observed the activities carried on by the spirits, I became aware of the fact that my prayers to the Lord Jesus had placed the demon spirits under some kind of restraint; they were limited in their capacities for destruction. They could not converse with me, as I believed they would have liked to do. I then commanded the spirits to leave, on the order of Christ Jesus, the Lord of glory. The lamp fell on the floor, as well as all the pictures that had been moved from their usual places. I picked up the lamp, straightened the damaged shade, but left the broken glass from the pictures to be swept up in the morning. I thanked the Lord Jesus in my heart for His loving care over me and returned to my bed.

A great sense of satisfaction came over me at the thought that powerful demon spirits left the premises on my command in the name of the Lord Jesus. That encounter also served to strengthen my conviction that everything was truly under control, as I had told my friend only a short while before. It must have been about an hour later when the spirits were back in action again. Once more, I commanded them to leave my place on the order of Christ Jesus the Lord of glory. Without hesitation, they left and I tried to get some sleep.

To my amazement, at about 4:00 A.M., their irritating behavior was repeated. I sat up in bed and tried to figure out why the Lord allowed the spirits to return. I concluded that maybe I should hear for myself how demon spirits felt about my accepting the Lord Jesus as my Lord and Savior, seeing that my friend Roland was so shaken over what the spirits had told the satanic priest. I opened conversation with a spirit.

"So, you want to talk to me? OK, speak up. What do you have to say?"

"Why do refuse to talk to us?" asked the spirit in a voice that moved about the room.

"I have found a better master."

"Why have you given us up," replied the spirit, "when we have great wealth prepared for you?"

"You have deceived me for so many years, as well as my whole ancestry, and I have no use for you."

"We have treated you right since you have affiliated yourself to that progressive group of individuals who know the real source of wealth and power," said he, in a voice that commanded respect and authority. I perceived that I was conversing with a chief counselor. In reality, the very air in the place was charged with energy. His presence was imposing, and I realized that I was no match for that power. Then, in my mind, I visualized my great High Priest, Christ Jesus.

I said within myself, *Lord Jesus, please help me!* Then two beautiful and powerful verses of Scripture came into my mind; verses that Pastor Taylor had brought to my attention that very day. *"He came unto his own, and his own received him not. But as many as received him, to them gave he power to become the sons of God, even to them that believe on his name"* (John 1:11, 12). Immediately, I felt that the Spirit of God would carry me through that encounter victoriously. A great calm came over me, and I became bold in the Lord.

As our conversation went on, and by the grace of the Lord Jesus, I was sustained in my determination to resist the spirit and to confess Christ Jesus as my only Master and Savior. I detected a crisis situation on the part of the spirit. In fact, I sensed waves of despair engulfing the spirit as he became aware that he was wasting his efforts in trying to regain my allegiance. I got the impression that a demotion was awaiting him if he failed in his diplomacy, as pertaining to this particular assignment.

"Listen to me attentively," said the spirit. "I am telling you the truth. The master has great wealth prepared for you if you only give up associating with the people he hates, and that seventh-day Sabbath he despises."

"Spirit, I believe you are telling the truth as pertaining to your wealth, but I don't want it, none of it. It's not enough. I have had a better offer for my allegiance; all the gold I want, plus a hundred million years of life to enjoy it; and I was told that is just the beginning of the good life. In fact, I am not interested in possessing gold or silver in this present world. I have decided to turn my life over to Christ Jesus. To serve Him is now the interest of my life."

"Stop mentioning that name," said the spirit counselor. "I need to talk to you, but don't mention that name. I am a chief counselor; my spirit associates and I have worked preparing the way so that the master could benefit your life with wealth. We have brought George the fame and honor he is now enjoying. We have arranged for you to make his acquaintance, so that you can understand that our interest and plans for your life are in like manner glorious. Don't pass up the wealth the master is offering you; I plead with you, don't pass it up."

"Spirit, I want you to know that ten days ago, I would have fallen for your line of glory, but not today; I am now what you could call an educated former demon worshiper. Jesus is now my Master; and by His grace, I will be a commandment keeper, and I will join those Sabbath keepers you hate. Now, one more point I want to bring to your attention, you and your spirit friends are in reality a bunch of cheats. You are offering me gold today, if I will forfeit the rights given me by the world's Redeemer to eternal life. Forget it, I can wait for the coming of the Lord, then I will possess all of your gold in the earth made new."

For about two minutes, there was perfect silence in the room. The only thing indicating activity was my alarm clock ticking away. I realized that tension was building up for the spirit counselor. Those two minutes of time led me to understand that the spirit counselor had met the unexpected. And as a losing general on a battlefield, he needed a little time to work out a new strategy.

"Very well," said the spirit. "You are refusing wealth and fame from the master, so it will be that poverty shall be the lot of your life. That is, if you manage to stay alive any length of time. You will from this day on walk under the shadow of death. We are experts in the work of bringing about misery and destruction in the lives of poor mortals."

Those words were then followed by a laugh such as I had never heard in my living days. I thought immediately that this must have been the type of laugh put forth by Nero, the emperor of Rome, when the lions were pouncing on scores of Christians he had commanded to be sent into the arena to be killed. A shiver went up my spine, and I probably would have been terrified to the highest degree possible, except that the Spirit of God blessed my mind immediately with the assurance that if one strikes the doorpost with the blood of Calvary's Lamb, he or she can rest in perfect peace from the hand of the destroyer. I will recount my experiences in chapters to follow.

"Spirit," I said in answer to his last statement of the conversation, "I want you to know that I have placed myself in the care of the Life-Giver, the Christ of Calvary, and I am prepared to walk under the shadow of death as long as the Sabbath-keeping Christ walks with me, by the presence of His Spirit. Now I command you in His name to depart from me and come no more."

There was a door that opened to a back balcony; it was opened as the spirit left, and slammed against the wall of the room with such force that the door handle almost went through the plaster. The first part of my command was carried out with great haste, but I was surprised to find that in the nights ahead, the spirits kept coming back. I was not aware of the fact that, in reality, they had an open invitation to my place, until Pastor Taylor made me mindful of it a few days later. I had in my apartment, on a closet shelf, a number of items that had been used in the conjuring of demon spirits. After those items were removed and disposed of, I had no more trouble. But until that time, I feared for my life.

Chapter 17

Ten O'Clock: The Episode of Death

I woke up Sunday morning to a new way of life. As I opened my eyes, becoming aware that another day had arrived, instead of reaching for a pack of cigarettes on the night table, which had become a deeply established habit of mine, I realized that I had no desire for the weed.

A surge of happiness filled my heart at the thought that I had a powerful new Friend in the Person of Christ Jesus, the Lord of glory, who had blessed my life in performing a miracle of love. In addition, I thought of the mighty way in which the Spirit of God had blessed my mind, and sustained me during my episode with the spirits but a few hours before.

I immediately raised my heart in thanksgiving to my great High Priest, Lord Jesus, in the Holy of Holies of the heavenly sanctuary. This took place while I was still lying in bed. I didn't want to do anything to interrupt my establishing an early rapport with my Lord that day, not even by changing position in bed. I conversed with Jesus in prayer, asking Him for guidance that day, because I realized that in a couple of hours I would be conversing with my friend, Roland, on matters of solemn importance. I was also aware that the power of demon spirits would again be encountered in some form or another.

I asked the Lord to brace me up with endurance for the conflict, so that I would not fall apart, realizing my human frailty. In the past, the power of association had led me to make bad decisions; I had given in many times to the suggestions of that one friend in particular. His reasoning had gradually led me into spirit worship. I was full of self-distrust.

During my conversation with the Lord, I didn't utter a word. I had become aware of the fact that demon spirits cannot intercept a silent prayer to God; I wanted to be one step ahead of my enemies. I felt a great satisfaction in keeping them guessing. And I felt honored that I, an undeserving human being, could open a conversation with the Most High, the mightiest Being in the universe, and demon spirits couldn't understand what was being communicated.

I continued my conversation with the Lord by telling Him that I didn't know where to begin in explaining to my friend about eternal realities; and he probably wouldn't be willing to listen because he wouldn't want to offend the spirits. Above all, how was I to withstand the pressures to come?

I paused a few seconds, and as I did, again the two beautiful and powerful verses of the Gospel of John 1, came to my mind, "He came unto his own, and his own received him not. But as many as received him, to them gave he power to become the sons of God, even to them that believe on his name" (verses 11, 12). I then felt that the Spirit of God would carry me through that encounter victoriously.

Without my realizing it, my request of the Lord was partly answered there and then. On my night table was my Bible. I reached over and began to shuffle the pages with one hand, then opened the Bible without paying attention. On those two pages of Scripture was resting the power that would literally save my life, by filling murderous hearts with a fear of the God of heaven, the Life-Giver, and thus immobilize hands that were ready to shed my blood.

A short while later, I decided to get up. When the time came to have my morning devotions, I picked up the Bible and began to read where it had been opened, at Isaiah 37. I read where a king by the name of Hezekiah had received a very distressing letter from a fellow with a big mouth by the name of Sennacherib, a hotshot who thought a great deal of himself. I was very impressed with the way the Lord handled the situation, and I received additional confidence in the thought that I really didn't have to worry about what was ahead. I couldn't help being concerned, but I should not worry.

At the time agreed upon for our meeting, my friend arrived. He looked worn out and distressed. I couldn't help telling him, "You look worn out, man. Are you sick?"

"Morneau, you have almost shocked the life out of both George and me. We can't believe that you would be so unkind and so unappreciative of what George has done to benefit our lives that you would turn around and insult the master by refusing from him the wealth he has prepared for you."

"When did you hear about that?" I asked.

"At the wee hour of five thirty this morning, when George phoned me up after a chief counselor had told him about your stupid decision and of my having to talk some sense into your head, or you are going to lose it."

"I see where I must have upset that chief counselor quite a lot by throwing him out the way I did."

"What's this? Did I hear you say that you threw a chief counselor out? I don't get you, man."

"You have heard correctly; about four o'clock this morning I had a conversation with a chief counselor, and when he became nasty, I had the Spirit of God throw him out. He left his mark on the wall when slamming the door open against it." I pointed to the indentation made by the doorknob.

"You—you, Roger Morneau, had a conversation with a spirit counselor. Do you know that some of our members have been worshiping and conjuring spirits for many years and haven't had the privilege of conversing with a chief counselor? And you have been dealing with the spirits but a short while, and you are accorded that great honor. This shows you how much the master thinks of you."

His face then changed to expressing excitement as he proceeded to say, "Morneau, you and I have a fantastic future awaiting us; now forget that bit about religion and let's go and see the high priest, and he will get you back in the favor of the spirits again and all will be well. The priest understands he doesn't hold anything against you for looking into religion, he likes you and understands you; he realizes that you are an adventurer by nature. He sees it's natural for you to search out a better way for yourself.

"The only thing the priest feels bad about is that if you were going to look into religion, why didn't you choose some other denomination instead of those Sabbath people, the very people the master hates most on the face of the earth? Man, you don't understand how much you have upset the gods—but I have the assurance of the high priest that all will be well if you come with me now, to see him at his office; he is there waiting for us. So, what do you say we go right now, old buddy?"

He then pulled out his pack of cigarettes and offered me one, which I declined, adding that I didn't smoke anymore. My friend was surprised, and couldn't help saying, "Morneau, you are a changed person; I could tell the moment I walked in here. I believe your very personality has changed. To be honest with you, I feel uncomfortable in your presence. You may find what I am going to say kind of foolish, maybe even stupid, but I feel out of place here with you, and I wish I were somewhere else. This is probably the way I would feel if I were in the presence of George VI, king of England."

As he was speaking those words, I realized that the Lord Jesus was fulfilling the words of the apostle John in my life. "He came unto his own, and his own received him not. But as many as received him, to them gave he power to become the sons of God, even to them that believe on his name." I felt that the glorious majesty of the Lord Jesus reflecting upon me created an invisible atmosphere of power unconsciously breathed in by my friend, causing him to react the way he did.

So I said, "What you are experiencing in my presence is because the Spirit that is with me is exceedingly greater in power and majesty than the spirit that is with you. And about your statement that I am a changed person, you are correct. I will never again be the Roger Morneau you have known to this day. In one short week, I have acquired knowledge concerning the ages eternal that is worth more to me than all the gold and silver planet Earth contains. This is why I cannot accept the wealth offered me by the spirits. In reality, if I did, I would be cheating myself.

"Don't get me wrong; I realize that the offer of wealth made to me by the spirits is a very generous one, but it lacks a most important element that should accompany it: *Life.* Yes, life in a measure sufficient to make that wealth worth possessing. I have been offered a better deal. All the gold I want, plus one hundred million years to enjoy it with; and I was told that this would be but the beginning of the good life."

Then I proceeded to set forth before his mind the glories of eternal realities. Though I lacked the capacity to bring forth a "Thus saith the Lord" in the manner that I had been instructed, the Spirit of God blessed my mind with the ability to put in my own words a message that held my friend spellbound for about forty-five minutes.

When I had covered those points that I felt needed to be set forth before him, and I paused to get some kind of response, all he would say was, "Now I understand." But he never asked any questions, and made no other comments. So I would get to talking again, and that continued for the period of time just mentioned.

Then he spoke up and said, "I can see where you don't intend to come with me to see the high priest. But you and I have to; you need to face reality again. All the wonderful things you have spoken about are not for you or I, so forget it; put it all behind you. First, I don't want to wait for the good life; I want it now. As for you, Morneau, you have no choice in the matter. You think you have, but you don't. You are kidding yourself by thinking that way. Morneau, you are not your own master; I wish you were, but you are not. The spirits own you in your entirety, and the sooner you acknowledge that the better off you will be."

The man became exceedingly agitated, and his whole countenance projected an air of impending doom. He got up and began pacing the floor, wringing his hands, then began to talk again.

"I am on an assignment most difficult for me to perform. What I am about to say to you I wish I were saying to my enemies, instead of to a longtime friend." He was by then perspiring profusely, although it wasn't warm in the room. Then it came out.

"Morneau, your days are numbered; along with those of the young couple who have been instrumental in leading you away from the master. However, I must tell you that you can put a stop to that plan of destruction initiated by the spirits by coming with me to see the high priest right now; he will restore you to the favor of the spirits and all will be well. In this way, no one gets hurt." He had to pause for a couple of seconds to use his handkerchief because perspiration was flowing down his face.

"One thing in particular the high priest wants to make you aware of, no one has ever gotten out of our secret society alive. You and I were brought into it by the special workings of the spirits, and we are to be in subjection to them, not they to us. Let me explain: up to now, you and I have felt that our meeting George in the way we did, and his inviting us to go to a restaurant for a snack, was by chance. Wrong—it was not sheer luck that we made his acquaintance in the way we did. The night before, a spirit appeared to George during the sacred hour and told him to go with his wife to that particular séance. He would be meeting us, and was told about our having been in the merchant navy and other details. He was given in detail what to say and what to do. All this had been worked out by the spirits, even to the point of his wife being taken up in conversation with the spirit medium to the extent that she would let George go home by himself and have the Belangers drive her home later. So, my friend, let's get going; time is running late."

By then he had his hand on the doorknob, expecting me to follow his directive. I, pointing to a chair, suggested that he sit down for a few minutes while I explained why I wouldn't go to see the high priest. He refused to sit, stating that he couldn't stand the atmosphere of the place any longer, adding that in reality a supernatural presence foreign to him made it impossible for him to sit and relax.

I then continued by saying that the presence of the Spirit of God was assisting me in answer to my asking help from the Lord of glory earlier that morning, so that I could make intelligent decisions. I proceeded to invite him to break away from the power of demon spirits and affiliate himself to the superior power of the Most High God. I assured him of safe conduct in making the transition from the one power to the other.

Then I was impressed to go one step further and invite the whole group of past demon worshiping friends to make the transition with him to that greater power. Again, I stated that I could guarantee safe conduct to every one of them in making that move. Then I said, "You guys like attention and respect, I'll tell you what I'll do. I'll call my pastor and reserve seats in our sanctuary for the coming Sabbath service; choice seats, on both sides of the center aisle. I'll reserve one hundred places, enough to make sure that everyone will be well seated."

"Don't go to the trouble," he said. "I am satisfied where I am now." Again, he had to pause as he was about to say something to wipe off the heavy perspiration running down his face. He continued, "And I know the other fellows feel the same as I do."

"Well, I felt the need to offer all of you the benefits of eternal life so that no one is left out." Then I changed the subject and returned to the ultimatum given me. "You are telling me that my days are numbered, along with those of my new-found friends, and that demon spirits intend to execute that sentence. Well, I have some news for you, the satanic priest, and all who entertain designs of mischief toward me and my friends.

"What I told a spirit counselor last night, I am saying again. I have placed my friends and I in the care of the Life-Giver, the Christ of Calvary. And I am prepared to walk under the shadow of death as long as the Sabbath-keeping Christ walks with me, by the presence of His Spirit."

My friend was actually shocked into a state of terror that deprived him for a couple of minutes of the ability to talk. He turned white as if the blood was leaving his face; his eyes became fixed, and I thought he was going to pass out. So I said, "Are you OK?" There was no answer. "Roland, is anything wrong with you?" No answer. Then within me, I said, *Dear Jesus, please help!*

He then shook his head and said, "I don't know what happened, but it seems as if I lost consciousness for a moment. Morneau, I know that the spirit accompanying you is very great and powerful; please don't mention it again, it terrifies me."

Again, he looked OK to me, and I mentioned that he should carry my message of refusal to the high priest.

"Morneau, I haven't made myself completely clear regarding the ultimatum. The threat on your life extends beyond what the spirits can do to you. The controlling committee has decided that your defection from our ranks could result in the leaking out of secret information, which would be damaging to the cause of the master. There was talk of having a contract put on you; one individual was willing to go as high as ten thousand dollars to have someone do away with you. The suggestion was thought unwise and was turned down.

"However, a decision was made that will be carried out; upon the information of a spirit that you have spoken to anyone on the outside regarding the activities of our secret society, three individuals have volunteered to shoot you at a convenient time. The controlling committee felt that this would be a wise move, seeing that all actions would be done from within our society, avoiding the possibility of becoming involved with the law.

"The plan was brought before a spirit counselor and received full approval, along with the gift of clairvoyance being given the volunteers so they would know where you are at all times, thereby being able to execute their assignment at the right time, in a quick and effective manner. I had hoped that I would not have to tell you this, but your refusal to comply with the high priest's wishes leaves me no choice but to bring all the danger facing you to your attention; I am sorry."

"Friend, I want you to go and tell the satanic priest that I am daring, but not stupid. I have nothing to gain by telling anyone about his secret society. Keeping my mouth shut, I can live with that. But my staying alive depending upon the word of a lying spirit, I will not stand for. Tell the old fox that I have a great deal going for him. I have a newfound Friend in the Person of Christ Jesus, the Lord of glory; He is great, all powerful, and commands respect. So much so that at the mention of His name, demon spirits tremble; and when commanded in that great name, even spirit counselors flee, as I experienced last night.

"My new Friend is the boss's Boss; in that all principalities and power owe their very existence to Him, and that includes the fallen Lucifer and all his demon spirits, even though they don't like to admit it."

I don't know if what I felt could be called righteous indignation, but that unjust design of the priest's woke up a determination in me to have him face the power and justice of God every remaining day of his life. I went on to tell my friend, "The priest seems to be knowledgeable regarding the Bible, tell him to look up Colossians chapter two, verses nine and ten; what I'm saying about the Lord of glory is there in black and white."

I jotted down the reference on a piece of paper so he would not forget, along with the one to follow.

"And while he has the Bible in hand," I added, "I have something else for him to consider. Centuries back, a powerful king went on conquering and bringing into submission to himself many great nations and people. But one day he insulted the wrong person. He attacked one who had made Christ, the Lord of glory, a very close Friend of his. As a result of the king's actions, 185,000 soldiers died; his whole army was turned into dead corpses, as says the Good Book. Sennacherib and a few of his officers were left alive to witness the results of his shouted insults and boasting. And when he arrived home in Nineveh, his two sons put a sword in his back. [Isaiah 37:1–38.]

"Roland, go tell the satanic priest that a great deal of thought should be given to the subject of doing away with Roger Morneau, lest the intended destroyers become the destroyed. They are taking on the Life-Giver, the Christ of Calvary who rose in glory. I will now lay down the rules of how the *game of extinction* will be played. And this I am doing with the full backing of my new Friend, who has revealed to me this morning how He intends to solve my problem."

Roland's eyes were as wide open as they could be, and I had his full attention. I walked over to the table where my Bible was open to Isaiah 37, and called him over to see something interesting. I had underlined in red those verses I intended to memorize (verses 14–20, 33–38). Showing him in written form the story I had just told him, I went on to tell how the Spirit of God had blessed my mind earlier that morning, causing me to open the Bible and become aware of how easily God could solve my difficulties. I read him a few verses.

His reaction was that of becoming very concerned over the whole matter when he said, "I can see where something like that could happen to us."

My reply was, "Yes, and that responsibility rests on the high priest." I continued, "Tell the man that the day he and his boys seriously entertain the idea of rubbing out Morneau, the Life-Giver, the Lord of glory, will pull the switch on all of his demon worshiping members, leaving him to be the only one alive so he can make the funeral arrangements. It could take place during one of their praise sessions to their false gods, when suddenly there will be dead silence."

By then my friend had sat down and lit himself a cigarette. After hearing these words, he began to shake, so much so that he couldn't place his cigarette on the ashtray. I had to walk over and do it for him.

"One more detail I want to cover with you, then I will let you go; the funeral arrangements. To help the priest handle the situation, here is a little advance help. Instead of his calling seventy funeral homes to remove bodies, it would be far preferable to call the Montreal Fire Department. If he explains himself correctly on why he needs their help, they could remove the ladders and firefighting equipment from a couple of large trucks, then all the corpses could be removed in hardly any time at all.

"The only embarrassing part of the game for him will be to give the *Montreal Star* and *Le Presse* accurate information on what happened and how it was brought about so that the newspaper headlines and articles will not make him appear as if he is responsible for it, deserving of incarceration or even execution."

By then my friend had heard enough on how the game of extinction was going to be played, and was back holding the doorknob in his hand, his countenance expressing a certain anxiety to leave.

"Morneau, I have to go; I'm afraid that what you have just told me may take place if no one else but the priest knows about it. So, I am going to phone George as soon as I leave here and tell him about all of our lives being in danger unless we stop those three self-appointed executioners. If the news gets to all the members before the priest has a chance to swear me to secrecy, there is a chance that the pressure exerted on him to call off the plan to silence you with a gun will be great enough to guarantee you a long life; that is what I intend to do."

As I shook his hand for the last time, he stated that because he wanted to avoid displeasing the spirits, we should avoid meeting again. Even to the point of ignoring one another's presence if by coincidence we met anywhere.

My reply was, "Have it your way."

In that manner ended a tension-filled trip into the supernatural and the loss of a close friend. But the benefits gained by my breaking away from it all, by the grace of the Lord Jesus, have been many to this day, and will be evaluated correctly only through the times eternal. The fact that I'm still alive today testifies to the goodness, love, and power of the Lord Jesus to save to the uttermost those who come to God by Him.

I never met that friend again, but I saw him from a short distance once as he came out of a store on Saint Catherine Street West, getting into his illegally parked Cadillac, sporting a white hat and what appeared to be a silk suit. He was impressive to look upon, but I didn't envy him.

As I walked down the street on that beautiful June day in 1947 to take a streetcar, my joy in the Lord was great and I raised my heart to the Holy of Holies of the heavenly sanctuary, and conversed with my newfound Friend, the Lord Jesus; and I truly considered that experience as being fullness of life.

Although I had turned my back on the spirits and all they had to offer, they kept trying to reestablish contact with me. Rappings took place almost every night and continued for months.

One evening Cyril came to observe; after his hearing the spirits rapping, he said, "Let's get out of here. How can you stay in this place? Why don't you move out?"

Somehow I didn't want to give the spirits the satisfaction of thinking that their actions were causing me to run from them. I figured that if I starting running from the spirits now, I would be running forever; unless I found a way of getting away from planet Earth. That was not feasible, so I had to play it cool. I trusted in the Lord Jesus and His being able to rebuke demon spirits by the power of the Spirit of God, and thus afford me the help and protection I needed so greatly.

Chapter 18

Counting My Blessings

The surprise

That Sunday morning ten o'clock appointment with my friend Roland had been a big surprise for both of us. After he left my place, I reviewed in my mind what had transpired during that meeting of ours. A surge of joy filled my heart as I realized that Christ Jesus, the Lord of glory, had so preciously heard my early morning request for help and had provided by His Spirit in a most marvelous way that help, guidance, and power that braced me up with endurance, which carried me through that episode so victoriously.

I then sensed a deep need of acquainting myself with the Word of God, by committing to memory verses that would maintain in my heart hope and courage in the Lord, and provide me with spiritual guidance in times ahead. At that very moment, I picked up my pen and a piece of paper, and wrote down verses of Scripture to commit to memory. I put the paper in my coat pocket and began there and then to occupy my mind with a meditation of the Word of God, the Word of life.

What deliverance; what a precious hope; what a blessing to my life that morning had brought.

The escape

November first came, that day known to me for so many years as "All Saints' Day," and more recently through my affiliation with demon worshipers as "Samhain" (Summer's End), in their carrying on a tradition of the ancient Druids.

Had not the Spirit of God worked so marvelously in my behalf, in my having Bible studies the way I did, and accomplished the wonderful deliverance that was mine to enjoy, that day would have been vastly different for me, in that I would have undoubtedly been initiated into that spirit worshiping society.

Like a bird released from the snare of the fowler, springing forth in the direction of the sun with a sense of liberty that a freed captive alone could understand, so was my joy in the Lord and my realization of the fact that Jesus had put an end to my captivity to the spirits, and opened the way for my visiting many of His beautiful worlds in the galaxies, through the eternal ages.

What deliverance; what a precious hope; what a blessing to my life.

A day that refreshes

On that first Sabbath, as I was about to leave the sanctuary, I asked the Lord to operate in my life with His redeeming grace, making it possible for me to find myself there again on the coming Sabbath. Yes, on that looked-forward-to Sabbath, I found myself entering that sanctuary, and being seated, I raised my heart to God in thanksgiving for His having worked so preciously in my behalf in the days just past. In fact, the whole day was a day of rejoicing in the Lord and of counting my blessings.

I then found by experience that there is a great benefit to be realized by a person reviewing, or counting, one's blessings. The commandment to remember the Sabbath day to keep it holy I perceived to have been given in order to make it possible for humans to escape the constant demands of the temporal affairs of life, and thus have the time available to count one's blessings, and in that way be brought closer to the Creator and be refreshed both physically and spiritually.

What peace was brought to my life; what a blessing.

The search

After my confrontation with the spirits, and life for me had resumed a normal pace, I immediately turned my attention to searching out through the channels of ecclesiastical and secular history, how the Christian church became involved in Sunday observance, having given up the observance of the Bible Sabbath, and at the same time adopting the doctrine of the immortal soul, eternal torment, and so on.

Especially interesting to me were accounts of how a great many converts to Christianity from Mithraism retained their belief in the doctrine of the immortal soul, along with the zeal they had for the day of the sun, mainly during the years of the Emperor Constantine, when it became fashionable to adopt the Christian religion.

For a period of five months, almost all my leisure time was occupied at the municipal library in Montreal. I read with great interest the writings of the Roman Catholic Church in the light of Bible prophecy. I looked into the lives of people who were considered pillars of the early Catholic Church and their influence on Christianity. The history of popes took on a new meaning as I read on.

I was especially fascinated in reading about Origen of Alexandria, an early Greek theologian who lived between the years A.D. 185 and 252, who had succeeded over a period of forty years in uniting some of the philosophies of the eclectic schools of Neoplatonism with the doctrines of Christianity.

At that time, I felt most appreciative and thankful to God for the writings of the Roman Catholic Church openly declaring to have changed times and laws (Daniel 7:25), thus fulfilling the prophecies of the Word of God.

That period of research and study served to solidify my belief in the Bible, and was indeed a great blessing to my life.

Days to remember

One beautiful Sabbath day in April 1947, I had the blessed experience of being baptized by immersion, and became a member of the Seventh-day Adventist Church. On that same day, I made the acquaintance of a young lady by the name of Hilda Mousseau. After attending an evening meeting that day, as some of us were coming out of the church, Pastor Taylor stated that anyone going east could ride a couple of blocks with him as he was going to park his car for the night. Four of us took up his offer, and after reaching the pastor's destination, proceeded walking to take the tramway.

On the way, Hilda and I became acquainted, and a number of times after that walked to the streetcar together. It wasn't long before we found that we had much in common; our interests were much the same, likes and dislikes, and so on. After a while, we found ourselves going steady. That interest in each other grew to the point that one day I thought it would be a good idea to try convincing her that she should become my wife.

In those days, it was a major project for a fellow to ask a young lady to marry him. One had to consider what would be the right place and the right time. I had reviewed in my mind a number of times my plan of action, so that all would be favorable to producing the desired result: an affirmative Yes. I set my sights on a particular Sunday evening to bring forth that big question, "Hilda, would you marry me?"

That important question would have to be asked under relaxed conditions. Yes—that would be an ideal time to ask, while waiting for the night watchman to come and unlock the door for Hilda; an excellent time I thought. It always took two or three rings for the man to come, amounting sometimes to a ten minute wait, depending how far away he was in the building.

All live-in nurses had to be in by 11:00 P.M. The closer one came to that time, the shorter the wait. I had figured on 10:30 P.M. being the ideal. Hilda was then practicing her nursing skills at the Montreal Convalescent Hospital, and resided in the nurses' quarters of that hospital.

It was a beautiful June day. As planned, we had a very enjoyable Sunday afternoon and evening together, culminating in a tour of the City of Montreal in an open streetcar. A very refreshing experience after the rays of a blazing sun had left us by painting on the light-blue sky a message of beauty and glory, declaring a soon return.

After each stop, as the tramway car would pick up speed, Hilda's beautiful long blond hair would rise from her shoulders and float in the breeze, and her lovely blue eyes would sparkle as they reflected the light of the many neon signs we encountered along the way. And the more I looked into her sweet face, the more convinced I became that her name should be Hilda Geraldine Morneau.

At about 10:30 P.M., we approached the entrance of the nurses' residence and, like many times before, Hilda pressed the bell button, and then kind of leaned her one shoulder against the door in the expectation of the usual long wait. It was then that I asked her if she would consider marrying me. No sooner had I spoken the words then the watchman appeared. He unlocked the door, stepped back about ten paces, folded his arms, and in the manner of a devoted servant to the well-being of the nurses, looked at me with an air that seemed to say, "I dare you to give her a good-night kiss in my presence."

Hilda was taken by surprise by both my question and the quick arrival of the usually slow-moving watchman. She stated that she had had thoughts on the matter, with an expectation of it taking place in a distant future. I assured her that all I was looking for at the time was a yes answer, and the agreement could become a reality at a later day, at a time convenient to her.

No sooner had I spoken that sentence, then watchman barked out, "Young lady, are you coming in, or do you want to stay out there? I've got work to do, and if you don't come in, I will lock the door with you out."

Dear Hilda gave me a quick yes, a peck of a kiss, and rushed in almost in tears. Again, the man spoke up, saying, "I'm going to teach you girls that when I unlock the door, it's for you to come in then."

"It's not every night," said Hilda, "that a girl is asked by a fellow to marry him."

"I'm sorry," said the watchman. "Why didn't you tell me it was that important? I would have given you more time."

It was too late for the man to teach Hilda when to come in. She determined there and then that she was moving out. Her mother, Mrs. Ann Mousseau, had a lovely apartment at the time on Queen Mary Road, and she was going to move in with her, regardless of how far she would have to travel to work.

While that interesting conversation was taking place, I was going home, realizing that my timing had been way off.

Charmed by Darkness

As soon as Hilda could reach a phone, she called her mother to inform her of her plans.

"Mother, I have something wonderful to tell you."

"You do? What is it about?"

"I am going to get married."

"Are you out of your mind? You're only twenty-one. Besides, who are you going to marry?"

"I am getting married to Roger, that young man from church I have been going out with; you know, the one you met a couple of times."

"Yes, but you have known each other only a short while. Aren't you rushing things a little?"

Then, according to Hilda, the fountain of tears let loose and she began to cry her heart out. The conversation then closed by her mother saying that there was no need of crying and they would talk things over the next time they were together.

The next evening I called my sweetheart, who informed me of her mother's viewpoint on the subject. I suggested that we both go and visit her mother on the coming Sunday and I would ask her for Hilda's hand in marriage. We would discuss that important matter with her and work things out to a satisfactory conclusion. It would then be possible to set a date for the great event that would be suitable to all parties involved.

It turned out that her mother was very understanding concerning our intentions, and September 20 was chosen for the wedding; the time, 9:00 P.M., on a Saturday evening. Actions that appeared for a while to bring nothing but distress, turned out to bring an abundance of joy.

It wasn't long before summer had given place to autumn, and the latter was out to outdo its predecessor in warmth, beauty, and charm. I rose early that Sabbath morning to discover that all of nature was vibrant with life. In a cloudless sky, the sun was fast at work in fulfilling the will of the Creator toward the human family, and in making that day a day to remember.

By the time we came out of church after the morning Sabbath services, the thermometer had reached eighty degrees. A few dry leaves were floating in a gentle breeze, as if to announce that they were no longer needed to shade the city folks, and therefore were coming down to rest from their fluttering activities so faithfully performed during the months just past.

Friends of ours by the names of Ruth and Arthur Cheeseman had opened their home to us for the wedding ceremony. It was planned to be a quiet, pleasant occasion with a few close friends attending. Among the guests were the Adventist clergymen and their wives, Pastor Andre Rochat, minister of the French church, and Pastor L. W. Taylor, minister of the English church, who officiated at the ceremony.

Mrs. Cheeseman, Mrs. Mousseau, and other ladies had arranged the home beautifully for that joyous occasion. As my lovely bride and I were before the pastor repeating our marriage vows, I stood tall and straight. Not as to impress any of the friends present, but to make the right impression on the many invisible personalities looking on; angels that had come from the presence of the Almighty on the one side, who were rejoicing with us, and demon spirits who were commanded by their heartless leader, who had seen their diligent efforts turn into failure when the grace of the Lord Jesus had walked out of their ranks.

Besides, I was wearing my very best suit of clothes. It was the tailor-made one bought with money acquired by the workings of demon spirits when I was playing the horses at the bookies.

So it was that another Christian home was established by the power of God's love. What a lovely occasion that was; what a day to remember; what a blessing to my life.

She lit up my life

I had never thought that married life could be so pleasant and enjoyable. Everyday brought some new interest and discovery. For instance, I recall that on one particular day as we were having our evening meal, and I was complimenting my bride on her excellent cooking, she manifested her appreciation of the compliment by asking what food was there that I hadn't eaten in a long time and would enjoy having.

"Hilda, dear," I said, "there is one food I used to enjoy a lot, and have not had in a long time—mashed turnip. My mother used to make the best mashed turnip I ever ate; if you could come up with something like it, I would enjoy it so."

On the following Sunday, as I was involved reading a good book, I heard my wife on the phone calling her mother for help.

"Mother, I have bought a turnip to cook for my hubby, and I don't know how to remove all that wax there is on it. Do you know how to remove it?"

From what her mother told me later, her reply was, "Dear daughter, unless someone has come up with a better way of doing it, the easiest way is to take the peel off the turnip with a knife."

The next thing I knew, my wife appeared in the living room with the turnip in one hand and a butcher's knife in the other, then said, "If you help me by peeling the turnip, I will cook you that favorite vegetable of yours."

How precious

This brief account of my life being benefited by the power of God's love at the beginning of my Christian experience is in reality but a glimpse of the Lord's love and care that was to multiply itself many, many times over in my behalf through three decades.

Chapter 19
Walking Under the Shadow of Death

It is not difficult to walk under Satan's shadow of death, as long as the Lord of glory disperses that shadow with the bright rays of the Spirit of life. While demon worshipers did not carry out any of their evil designs against me, demon spirits attempted to take my life an innumerable number of times over the years.

Because of a deep sense of appreciation of the preciousness of life, prompted mainly by the fact that in the back of my mind has ever been present that declaration of a demon spirit that their attention would ever be focused upon me as a choice subject to exterminate, it has led me to raise my heart to God in thanksgiving as soon as I awake each morning. I have sought God's loving care over my wife and me, along with our children, and those early morning petitions have been heard and honored greatly over the past decades.

For more than twenty years, my work has caused me to travel in cars anywhere between thirty to forty thousand miles per year, which has exposed me to the possibility of becoming part of the yearly statistics of highway fatalities.

I have traveled in rainstorms, snowstorms, dense fog, and other unfavorable travel conditions. I have seen cars coming at me that were driven by drunks, or individuals with their minds spaced out on drugs, or persons whose minds were under the influence of demon spirits. But in answer to those early morning prayers, the Spirit of God blessed my mind a great many times, causing me to make the right move at the right time, and thus escape destruction. I have had too many close calls to remember them all.

At this time I wish to recount a half dozen instances where I feel demon spirits were highly instrumental in working out what could have been the end of life for me, my wife, and children, and also for Cyril and Cynthia, just after my having been baptized into the commandment-keeping church.

The horse incident

It was late March, in the early sixties. We had had a lot of snow that winter in the western New York area. In Wyoming County, especially around the Arcade region, snowplows had built up snow piles on either side of roads reaching at times as high as ten feet.

The rigor of winter was beginning to abate, as the sun was gaining strength, and the days were getting longer. Everyone was looking to better days ahead as nature was indicating a change to spring weather.

On one particular evening at about nine o'clock, I was traveling a rural road in the vicinity of Rushford, New York, at a reasonable rate of speed, slowing down before entering turns in the road because it was impossible to see if any vehicles were coming around the corner because of the high snow banks blocking the view.

After a while, I suddenly came upon a stretch of road quite slippery because some of the snow had thawed during the day and the resulting water had frozen when the sun went down, leaving large patches of ice and making it impossible to reduce my speed by braking, because it would have been exceedingly dangerous to lose control of the car. I touched neither brake nor accelerator, but let the car roll into a sharp curve with the hope that nothing was coming from the opposite direction.

Around the curve I went, then my eyes focused upon the unbelievable; across the road stood a large horse and I had no choice but to hit that horse. By then the car had slowed down to about twenty miles per hour, but at any speed a person can be killed by running into such a large animal. One quick decision I had to make: Which end of the horse should I drive into?

Like other near disasters I had encountered, I cried out, "Dear Jesus, please help!" Instantly, without my thinking what to do, the car was steered into the direction of the front legs of the horse; when I was close to impact, the horse rose up on his hind legs and I passed under the front ones, barely clearing the windshield and the top of my car.

I was then able to bring the car to a stop a short way down the road, giving my pounding heart a couple of minutes to recover from the terrifying experience, and at the same time to send forth a prayer of thanks to my precious Redeemer.

Realizing the danger to other motorists encountering that horse, I drove to the first house down the road to see if it was theirs. Having told the man of the house the details of my encounter and describing the animal, he informed me that it was undoubtedly the neighbor's and was kept indoors during the winter months.

He picked up the phone and rang the owner to inform him that his horse was out of the barn. After he hung up the phone, he stated that the farmer was going to check on the horse, who was seen in his stall about a half hour before, at the time the man had completed his evening chores; he would call right back.

A few minutes later, the phone rang, and the message came that the stall door was wide open and the horse was gone; the farmer couldn't figure out how the horse had gotten out. I understood, and again my heart was lifted up in a prayer of thanksgiving to God for His tender loving care over a most undeserving human being.

At Sears' parking lot

In December 1971, I was working on the telephone directory of Watertown, New York. A few mornings had been exceedingly cold for that time of the year, and I wanted to assure myself that my DieHard battery would not fail me in a morning start; so I proceeded to the Sears & Roebuck Auto Department to have someone check that battery out.

It was a busy morning in that service department, and it took a while before someone could attend to my needs. Being unable to bring the car indoors as the bays were full, the service manager brought a tester out to the car, performed the needed check, and assured me that the battery would carry me through the winter without any problems.

Meanwhile, a large tractor trailer truck loaded with twenty-seven tons of cargo had been parked right behind my car, and the driver had gone into the store to get unloading instructions. My car was facing the building, and I couldn't get out.

At the time, I was driving a small Saab automobile, model ninety-six. The fellow that had checked my battery suggested that I back under the body of the trailer because there was sufficient room to do so and he would guide me in my move. It sounded like an excellent suggestion. The truck motor was turned off, and the brakes were well engaged, otherwise it would have rolled down the hill, because the parking lot was on a steep incline.

Getting into the car, I started the motor, placed the gear shift in reverse, and slowly backed under that huge cargo box. I was backed up as far as I needed to, and the man was motioning me to steer to the left and out, when suddenly I sensed that same feeling of urgency that in times past had led me clear of destruction so many times.

I quickly placed the car in first gear and shot right back into that parking place; but not fast enough to avoid being hit by a wheel of the truck that knocked out the light off the end of one of the rear fenders. I jumped out of the car in time to see that huge truck race backward down the hill, colliding with cars and jackknifing to a stop as it demolished the back half of a large Chrysler automobile.

The driver of the truck appeared on the scene in time to see his vehicle hit that last car. He couldn't believe his eyes. He declared with great earnestness that he had the truck in forward gear and that the emergency or parking brakes were on and well secured.

The owner of that last damaged automobile was furious. He and his wife had gotten out of the car about two minutes before the accident took place and were walking up to the store when they saw it all happen. He began to accuse the driver of the truck of being many things unflattering, including being an idiot for leaving a truck standing without the parking brake on; he was going to check out those brakes there and then.

The driver refused to let anyone enter the cab of the truck, and stayed out of it himself until the Watertown City Police could get there and make an accident report. A few minutes later the police arrived, and after listening to an account of what had taken place, one of the officers climbed into the cab of the truck and looked over the controls.

All present listened attentively to the officer who, having a clipboard in one hand and a pen in the other, began to write his findings:

1. Ignition Switch: Off.
2. Gearshift: In neutral position.
3. Parking Brake: Secured; red light on instrument panel indicating "Brake on" when ignition switch is turned on.
4. Malfunction inexplicable.

The police officer came down from the cab asking to talk to the individual whose car was hit first. As I stepped forward stating that I was he, the officer went on saying, "Did I hear the service manager correctly, that he advised you to back your car under that trailer?"

"Yes, officer, it was an unwise move on my part, and I shouldn't have done it."

Having asked for my driver's license, and as he was writing down the information he needed, he said, "Mr. Morneau, you are a very fortunate to be alive. I am sure you are aware that one second longer under that truck and you would not be here making an accident report. That little car of yours would have been flattened to the pavement with you in it. Some people are just plain lucky, and I see that you are one of those."

"Sir, I am thankful to God for His protecting care over me. This is one of many instances in which my life has been preserved."

He handed me back my driver's license saying, "Let me shake your hand for good luck, maybe some of your good fortune will rub off on me."

As I got into my car, I asked the Lord to bless that officer's life with His tender, loving care, to benefit his life in the manner in which He had benefited mine, and to save him into His eternal kingdom. As for myself, again I thought back to 1946 and the conversation I had with a spirit counselor who had declared that demon spirits are experts in bringing misery and destruction into the lives of poor mortals, and that the days of my life would be but few.

At that same time, the Spirit of God had blessed my mind with the assurance that if one paints the doorpost with the blood of Calvary's Lamb, he or she can rest in perfect peace from the hand of the destroyer.

Yes, once again Satan's shadow of death had come very close to me, but the bright rays of the Spirit of life in Christ Jesus had dispersed that shadow in a moment of time. As I drove away, my heart was lifted up to my heavenly Father in thanksgiving for the power of His love having operated so marvelously in my behalf to that day, and for a fresh manifestation of His interest and care that was sure to accompany me through the remainder of my pilgrimage through the land of the enemy.

Pushed off the road

I was working on a telephone directory in the eastern part of New York State. Because a great many businesspeople had taken off on that beautiful Wednesday afternoon of July, I found myself making appointments with secretaries to handle the firm's Yellow Pages advertising on the following day. Thursday was going to be a real busy day, working on a tight schedule.

I rose a bit earlier that morning because I had to work in a phone call to a contractor at six thirty, to set a time convenient to meet with him because he was working on a project out of town and was difficult to meet up with.

During that phone conversation, the man informed me that I should see him an hour later, at seven thirty, because his work was taking him away for two weeks. I agreed to see him at the time mentioned and closed the conversation.

From that moment on, it was rush, rush, rush. My devotions were shortened with the thought of catching up with it after that first appointment. What I figured would be a straight renewal of the advertising, turned out to be quite lengthy. The firm had acquired a new logo, and the cuts in their ads needed to be replaced with more up-to-date ones, plus many changes had to be made in the copy. Those changes having been made, I realized that in a few minutes I should be at my next appointment, which was about five miles away.

I reasoned that if I could cancel that one appointment and reset it for late afternoon, or on the following day, I would then have the time to return to the motel, have my usual devotions, and get myself some breakfast. So I asked for the use of the phone and called what was in reality the first appointment of the day.

After getting the owner on the line, I explained that something had come up that made it difficult for me to see him at the time set the day before with his secretary and could I reset our meeting to another time that would be convenient to him. His reply was that he himself had changed his schedule for that day to accommodate the time set with me by his secretary and would wait for me even if I were late in getting there.

"I'll see you in a short while," I said and hung up the phone. Being mindful of keeping to the speed limit, I proceeded to the meeting, losing no time in getting there; again, hoping to be able to reset the following appointment. Having attended to the advertising needs of this customer, I asked to use his phone, and calling my next scheduled customer, was faced with having to keep the appointment. I asked for directions on how to get to his place of business, thanked him, and hung up.

I got into my car and took off, keeping my mind on the landmarks he said to watch for and the names of roads to turn onto. It meant traveling over a few hills in order to get to that valley. Taking a quick look at a road map, I felt that the man had given me a roundabout way of getting to his place. The directions consisted of state roads, which were probably the ideal way to travel there, but I thought that if I could use some secondary roads shortening the distance, it would save me some time.

Stopping at a service station, I asked if there were any shorter way of getting to my destination.

"Yes, there is," said the attendant, "if you go about one mile down this road and take a left turn on county road number __, it will get you over the hills without any problem; it's a good road, paved all the way." Having spoken those words, he looked up into the sky, then said, "It looks like we may get a shower or two; look at those angry clouds building up. If it rains while you're traveling that way, be careful of the turns in the road, some of them have no guard rails."

I thanked him and left. About ten minutes later, it started to rain with such intensity that I had to stop and wait for the downpour to end. A short while later, as suddenly as it had begun, the rain stopped. I proceeded down the road with caution, enjoying the response of my new automobile in its quick acceleration after my having reduced the speed considerably to negotiate some of the turns in the road. Then suddenly, I experienced strange actions on the part of my car.

I was on level ground coming to a bend in the road, broken up by a bridge with no guard rails securing its entrance; a road sign with the familiar arrow indicating a sharp bend suggested thirty miles per hour as a safe speed to observe. Because of the wet pavement, I was careful in making that turn, moving at twenty miles per hour to be doubly safe.

As I entered the bend steering the car to the right, it didn't respond but continued straight ahead; I slammed on the brakes with great force. I felt them taking hold, but the car didn't slow down. As a couple of the wheels slid off the pavement onto the shoulder of the road, the brakes locked completely. The rolling of the gravel and the squealing of rubber on the pavement made a terrifying noise, and

I realized that the car was being pushed by some invisible force.

I shouted, "Dear Jesus, please help!" Instantly, the car stopped; and I sat perfectly still for a few minutes thinking about my predicament. How could I get out of the car without making it go over the edge to a rocky riverbed some fifty feet below? From where I was, I couldn't tell how close the front wheels were from sliding down the embankment, but what I could see of my environment indicated it was too close for me to be comfortable sitting there.

Leaving the motor running, I placed the gearshift in park position, secured the emergency brake, then slowly opened the door and got out of the car. What a near disaster I was looking upon; another ten inches and the front wheel on the driver's side would have been in the void, and I could imagine the car tumbling down to the riverbed with my being in it.

In a very careful way, I got back in the car, left the door open, and backed up my vehicle to safe ground. I then lifted my heart to God in thanksgiving for the power of His love and grace. That incident served to make me mindful once again of the fact that my supernatural enemies weren't giving up on their intentions to bring me to an early grave. On the other hand, it reinforced my conviction that the superior power of my precious Redeemer was ever present to assure me shelter and deliverance from the hand of the destroyer.

The vanishing dog

I got up at four o'clock that morning to go to work. It being late fall, I took a quick look outside to see if there was any fog to contend with that day. We were living only three miles from the Letchworth State Park, better known to some people as the Grand Canyon of the East. The huge gorge cradles the Genesee River, which at times can be the cause of dense fog covering the valley for miles.

Yes, my fears were confirmed; fog had developed. The mercury light spreading its illumination over our yard seemed to do so in half its capacity. The fog was dense and uninviting; closing the door, I decided to take a few additional minutes for morning devotions.

At about five thirty I took off, regardless of the fog and prompted mainly by a declaration of Scripture, "He that observeth the wind shall not sow; and he that regardeth the clouds shall not reap" (Ecclesiastes 11:4). And I felt that fog had a similar application here, as relating to my earning a living.

Proceeding down the road at about forty miles per hour, I tried to exercise prudence in keeping a speed that would allow the car to stop readily if something unexpected presented itself. Above all, my reliance upon God's loving care was reassuring, and afforded a measure of safety that I came to rely upon under unfavorable conditions such as experienced that morning.

Like many times before in driving to work in snowstorms or fog, I asked my great High Priest, Christ Jesus, to bless my mind by the power of His grace with a sense of oncoming danger, were I in a position of driving into a vehicle or anything that would involve me in an accident.

Having the headlights dimmed and my eyes focused on that reflecting centerline assured me of being on the right side of the road. I was heading east on Route 70, with the intention of getting on the southbound expressway at Hornell, New York. Of highest importance in all my concerns was the intersection of Routes 70 and 36, called a "death trap" by the natives. Route 70 terminates in Route 36, with no great effort having been put forth on the part of the highway department to let people know that a very dangerous situation could develop unexpectedly for motorists coming to that intersection. Many bad accidents had taken place there in the past because of rain or snow making the pavement slippery, and vehicles slamming into the side of a hill not having had enough time to slow down to make the stop indicated by an ordinary sign stating, "Stop Ahead."

Coming out of the village of Canaseraga, I accelerated from the local speed to about thirty-five miles per hour and held it there, knowing that about three miles ahead was that dangerous intersection, and I wanted to make double sure that I saw that small sign indicating the stop ahead.

The fog wasn't getting any lighter, and all my attention was centered on my driving, when a large black dog approached my automobile and seemingly without effort, kept pace with the front fender of the driver's side. It seemed as if the dog wanted to race the car, as he would proceed a few feet ahead, then slow down to allow the car to catch up with him. *What a strange dog,* I thought. He had the body of a greyhound and the tail of an Irish setter, and could he ever run. At that moment, the dog was about six feet ahead of my car and turned his head to see how far back the car was.

I decided to see just how fast that dog could run; the speedometer began to climb: thirty-seven, thirty-nine, forty-two, and the dog didn't seem to mind the added speed. By then I had lost all thought of what was ahead. Pressing a little harder on the accelerator, the speed reached forty-four, forty-five, forty-seven, and then my mind was seized with a sense of oncoming danger that was terrifying, as the Spirit of God brought me back to reality.

I slammed on the brakes as hard as I could to slow that car down. Then I saw the stop sign and cried out, "Dear Jesus," but I didn't have the time to say "please help." With the four wheels locked, I skidded across Route 36 and came to a stop facing a solid wall of dirt. I placed the gearshift in reverse and quickly backed up out of the way and said a few words of prayer in thanksgiving to my Lord and Savior.

An angel of God must have stopped the car for me because it would have been humanly impossible to slow down and stop an automobile that way. Oh! The dog—he vanished when help from on high moved in.

Three weeks later, under similar fog conditions, a man died on that same spot when his tractor trailer truck loaded with milk slammed into the side of that hill.

On the Sabbath following my near disaster, I had the eleven o'clock service at the Adventist church in Wayland, New York; once in a while our minister who pastored three churches would have one of his local elders deliver the eleven o'clock message to one of the congregations. In my travel to Wayland, I had to cover that same stretch of road, which by now had become a monumental reminder of what the Lord had done to save me from the hand of the destroyer.

As I made the required stop at that intersection and saw the heavy tire marks left by my car on the pavement, realizing how close I had come to being killed, a deeper sense of appreciation of the goodness of the Lord was felt; and the joy of counting my blessings on that Sabbath was increased greatly.

That morning I shared the joy of my experience with God's Sabbath-keeping people, who rejoiced with me at the thought that in this day and age, we have the blessed assurance that the Lord is concerned with the well-being of His commandment-keeping people.

Watch out for that telephone pole!

In our home, my wife, Hilda, and I have established the principle of family devotions from the beginning of our married life, and our three children have had the benefit of being brought up hearing daily some of the great stories of the Bible that show God's loving care for those who call upon His great name.

Without trying to scare our children into serving the Lord, we have brought to them awareness—a sense of understanding of the fact that we are in our lifetimes pilgrims traveling through the land of the enemy. Also, that we should always be conscious of the fact that forces are at work to separate us from God and work out our destruction. If demon spirits can't separate us from the Lord, their frustration then turns into bitterness and hatred, which motivates them to seek means of bringing harm or even death to the Christian.

An understanding of those factors has helped us all to seek God's grace and care early each morning. And many have been the manifestations of God's redeeming grace in our lives over the years.

I'd like to illustrate what I have just mentioned by recounting a short experience that happened to my wife and our daughter Linda in 1962. It was late in the fall of the year, and unusually high winds had stripped trees completely of their leaves and brought down from the Arctic Circle those unwelcomed currents of air that had the ability to penetrate human flesh and chill one's very bones.

Arriving home from school one day, Linda's first words to her mother after closing the kitchen door were, "I can't stand that cold wind; and to make matters worse, the weatherman is forecasting an abundance of chilling rain for tomorrow. I wish I lived in the tropics."

Her mother, prompted by acquired knowledge gained by many years of living through some very cold seasons, suggested that the young lady proceed to an upstairs closet where comfortable clothing had been stored a few months back and reacquaint herself with the art of making oneself comfortable.

The suggestion was heeded and for a while seemed to be satisfactory until Linda appeared in the kitchen with a woolen skirt on that refused to be brought down to the knee, and with a heavy-duty raincoat whose sleeves appeared to have shrunk two or three inches. Modeling these items for her mother, Linda stated that there was nothing wrong with the garments except that she had grown too tall for them.

Without hesitation, it was decided that a bit of shopping was in order, and getting in the car, they proceeded in the direction of the big city—Buffalo. At the time our residence was in Curriers, New York.

At about 7:00 P.M., returning home from their shopping trip, they encountered a bad rainstorm that had battered the village of East Aurora with high winds for about two hours, leaving broken trees and branches everywhere. Visibility was very poor because of the darkness and a driving rain. As they left the village at a moderate rate of speed, they kept watching for the unexpected.

After a while, Linda saw what appeared to be a man waving his arms in a motion to stop. Realizing what was taking place, she yelled to her mother, "Watch out for that telephone pole!" Hilda slammed on the brakes just in time to avoid having the telephone pole fall on top of them. It ended up hitting a front corner of the car, damaging the bumper and fender.

According to a neighbor, some linemen had set that telephone pole up that same day, and having additional work to do, had left without securing it properly. The high winds and the heavy rain had caused it to shift out of place and it toppled over. Were it not for God's tender, loving care over the ladies, my loss could have been very great that day.

Escape from a wall of flame

As I have mentioned earlier, demon spirits had determined that Cyril's and Cynthia's lives should be shortly brought to an end for the part they had played in my breaking affiliation with the spirit society.

In order not to worry my young friends, I refrained from letting them know what the spirits had purposed to do to them. But every morning I brought their need of protection before the Lord, placing them under His loving care. And every Sabbath day, as I counted my blessings and rejoiced in the goodness of the Lord (which I am still doing), I never failed to thank the Master for His having held back the power of the destroyer from touching any one of us.

That carefree and joyous experience continued for about six months, then for some reason that we cannot explain in this present world, the Lord allowed a calamity to take place in the lives of Cyril and Cynthia, which brought great distress to them and almost cost Cynthia her life.

Demon spirits seized upon a bit of human carelessness. Having come close to death a number of times has led me to believe that such experiences are allowed to take place in a certain person's life to keep them mindful that their invisible enemies are ever ready to seize upon opportunities to end their life. It has a sobering influence on one's mind that makes it impossible to take life for granted. Above all, it draws one closer to his or her Redeemer.

A unique fire took place in my young friends' residence; the account of that incident I bring to you in Cyril's own words. But in order to understand the account correctly, we need to know a little about the setting of that living room where those precious Bible studies took place. The lines to follow are a continuation of Cyril's written account mentioned at the end of chapter 11.

> When Roger requested Bible studies for that very night, I went home and got out my *Brief Bible Readings for Busy People,* [and] we prepared the living room so that he would be comfortable. Since Cynthia, my wife, and I loved good music, we decided that our guest should be greeted with soft music in the background. For our first meeting, I decided not to use heavy church music, as I didn't want to scare him off by causing him to think we played only church music seven days a week. We do play fine classical music, and it was decided that on that October night when Roger entered, he would hear the soft strains of Ravel's *Bolero* playing on our large radio-record player combination.
>
> As he entered, he seemed tense; however, he liked the music and made a comment to that effect. After introductions, we sat down, relaxed, and after a while turned the music off and started our studies.
>
> Roger was like a hungry man starving to death, but his hunger was for the Word of God. Of course, we were delighted at his desire. . . .

Passing over Cyril's account of the Bible studies we had had, we will now hear his account of that fire they experienced.

> Roger has stated how the evil one tried to do him harm. Without realizing what was happening, we had a few frightful experiences also; one almost took the life of my wife, Cynthia.
>
> After Roger was baptized, one afternoon my wife and I were in the same room [where] we gave those most important Bible studies, when my brother-in-law decided to test the volatility of some cleaning fluid we had; he neglected to cover the can and in seconds the room was in flames. Cynthia was trapped behind a wall of flame, her only escape was through a window—but that was a drop of three stories; a drop that would have been fatal.

My brother (eleven or twelve years old) ran to call the fire department, as I ran to another room to get a blanket to beat the flames in order to save my wife; and in so doing I yelled for her to back away from the flames.

When I returned seconds later, the spot where Cynthia stood had exploded with such force that a hole was blown through the ceiling and the floor where she stood was burning red flame. The radio phonograph that [had] played the beautiful music [at] that first Bible study was reduced to ashes. I looked at the flaming room and realized that Cynthia was standing outside, beside me looking at the flames. The blanket I [had thrown] in was ashes.

Cynthia told me that something told her to jump. Her jump (which I am convinced was guided by the angels) carried her over the flames of that large radio to safety. The ends of the hair on her head were singed, her eyelashes were burned, but no skin on her body had been touched by the flames.

After the firemen put out the flames, we checked the room to see how much was lost. We found that everything in that room was burned. In a closet we had a suitcase with clothing inside. The suitcase was not touched by the flames, yet some of the clothing in the center was ashes while the rest of the clothing remained intact.

I attributed my wife's deliverance to the grace of God and to His promises, one of which is recorded in Psalm 91:9–14, "Because thou hast made the Lord, which is my refuge, even the most High, thy habitation; there shall no evil befall thee, neither shall any plague come nigh thy dwelling. For he shall give his angels charge over thee, to keep thee in all ways. . . . Because he hath set his love upon me, therefore will I deliver him; I will set him on high, because he hath known my name." My wife's mother taught her this beautiful psalm when she was very young, and today she still rejoices in its wonderful promise.

It encourages my heart to review briefly some of the instances that have served to keep me mindful of the great conflict continually going on between invisible agencies—the great controversy between the forces of good and evil.

The superior power of our great Redeemer preciously manifested in these instances serves to confirm that the decision I made in 1946, prompted by the Bible studies received in that one week, have indeed been sound and wise ones.

God is in verity my Refuge and Strength, a very present help in trouble.

Epilogue: A Ministry of Reconciliation

The account of my trip into the supernatural is now ended. But please don't close the book—I want you to become a blessing in the lives of a great number of people.

You may say, "I am too busy to get involved in anything that will demand more of my time; I have too many demands placed on me as it is."

So, I sympathize with you, and believe you. It's because you are an active, involved, and industrious person that I am appealing to you. Permit me to explain. I wish to interest you in a prayer ministry.

My having been from Satan's altar to God's mercy seat has given me a unique insight into the supernatural. Understanding the modes of operation by which demon spirits have been so very successful in separating humans from their Creator, and in causing poor mortals to destroy themselves and others with them, causes me to believe that all who are members of the family of God should dedicate themselves to carrying on a special ministry for one's fellow humans oppressed by demon spirits.

Sad to say, but the majority of Christians are unaware of the great extent to which that spirit oppression is carried, even when they are struggling with it in their own homes. I am thinking of the importance of placing sinners, the hopeless, the undeserving, the oppressed, in a position of freedom from the oppression of demon spirits; a position where they can make intelligent decisions regarding their well-being in this present life, and for eternity.

As Christian sojourners passing through the land of the enemy, you and I have capacities, or rights, that no one else can exercise, not even the angels of heaven. And God wants to make us channels for the outworking of the greatest force in the universe—the operation of the Spirit of God on behalf of perishing human beings.

We are called to work along with Jesus in restoring poor mortals to God's righteousness and, in so doing, enable them to obtain eternal life, which our heavenly Father is so freely offering to them (2 Corinthians 5:17, 18).

We should become involved in a special prayer ministry. Relief for the oppressed comes through prayers that are specific in nature. Too many Christians pray in generalities and because of that, never see their prayers answered before their eyes.

I have practiced what I am telling you, for many years, and to illustrate how it has worked for me in blessing the lives of others, I wish to recount a few instances in which the power of the Spirit of God rebuked the power of demon spirits operating in the lives of helpless humans, and brought to them the sweet peace of God's love.

Shocked into prayer

It was late in April 1972, and I was driving home from my week's activities in telephone directory work. I decided to stop in Watertown, New York, to pick up a couple of items needed. Having driven to the parking lot of the F. W. Woolworth store, I went in, bought what I had to get, then returning to my car decided to take a few minutes and process the paperwork that had to be done sooner or later.

It was a great day, in that the temperature had reached into the high seventies, and a gentle breeze seemed to revive nature with promises of yet greater and better things to come. Getting into my car, I quickly opened the windows to release that superheated air that proved uncomfortable to sit in. A few minutes later, a green Mercury automobile pulled in two parking spaces away from where I was.

Taking a peek from the corner of my eye, I saw a middle-aged couple with the woman at the steering wheel. As I continued working on my papers, I was shocked into prayer. A conversation took place between the two individuals that went like this:

"Mary, you will have to start the car so I can put up this power window."

"Jim, you are stupid; I have told you a hundred times that the windows have to be put up while the motor is running. Won't you ever learn?"

The man then opened up and brought out a mixture of the sacred and profane to get across to his wife that her words had reached a sensitive spot in his brain. He was getting very angry, accusing her of being instrumental in wrecking what had begun as a perfect day for him by refusing to keep her mouth shut.

Instantly, my mind was transported back to 1946, to a statement made by the old satanic priest that demon spirits delight in stirring up human emotions to heights sufficient to create anger or hatred capable of murder.

Immediately, within myself, I cried to my great High Priest, Christ Jesus, in the Holy of Holies of the heavenly sanctuary. "Dear Jesus, please forgive the iniquities and sins of these my fellow travelers; and by the mighty power of the Holy Spirit, rebuke the demon spirits that are oppressing their minds, and bless their lives with the sweet peace of Thy love."

Suddenly, the verbal storm stopped, and the sea of life became perfectly still for those two precious souls. For about one minute, not a word was spoken, then the man broke the silence by saying, "Mary, I'm sorry I got so angry, really, I feel bad now that I spoke to you the way I did. I don't know why I get so angry; at times I can actually feel hatred mount up in me toward people I dearly love."

Then it was beautiful to hear the woman admit that she was at fault to a great extent, in that she was not careful with her words; and at times actually took pleasure in jabbing him with pointed words. Promising to be more considerate in the future, she gave him a peck of a kiss on the cheek, and both got out of the car after putting the window up.

Stepping to the parking meter, the husband looked at his change to feed the meter, and having no dime or nickel, turned to his wife, saying, "Sugarplum, would you be kind enough to look in your purse for some change?"

"How can I refuse to help when you are treating me as a lady? Do you realize, Jim, that you haven't called me your sugarplum since the kids were little?"

After he deposited the coins in the meter, she grabbed him by the arm, and like two lovers they proceeded to do some shopping.

I, sitting in my car, had the surprise of my life, and a new dimension had been added to my Christian experience. Never before had I asked the Lord to forgive someone's sins. I had given the matter some thought, but that was as far as it had gone. And as I said a short while ago, I was shocked into that prayer.

When the verbal abuses started to fly, I discerned demon spirits at work oppressing the minds of those people, and as the sacred and profane were brought forth, I realized that the man probably hadn't had his sins forgiven in twenty years. Knowing that sin separates between God and man, I sensed the urgency of the moment and took action in asking the Lord Jesus for the grace that I was sure would bring those individuals the deliverance they needed, and the sweet peace of God's love to bless their lives.

As I continued reflecting on the incident, I discerned that the demon spirit's game of mind oppression had been brought to a stop by the mighty power of the Spirit of God breaking the forces of the tyrant, leaving the couple surrounded with the atmosphere of heaven; in reality, an ideal situation for anyone to find oneself in.

A Ministry of Reconciliation

I was amazed to see how quickly and how different the individuals' outlook on life became when they found themselves relaxing under the light of heavenly grace. And I had been instrumental in opening the way so the Lord Jesus could benefit their lives as He did. Also, that great change had taken place without my having opened my mouth, or getting on my knees. *How practical a ministry,* I thought. I was impressed—what a mighty power; what a mighty Redeemer we have in the Person of the Lord Jesus.

Was not this type of problem solving carried out by our Lord while on earth? I thought. *Of course it was!* To the paralytic who was hoping for physical healing, Jesus said, "Thy sins are forgiven thee" (Luke 5:20). First, the Lord removed from the helpless man his burden of sin; then did the next important thing, He healed him. Also, at Simon's house, when a woman seeking peace for her soul anointed the Master's feet with precious ointment, Jesus said to her, "Thy sins are forgiven. . . . Thy faith hath saved thee; go in peace" (Luke 7:48, 50).

From that moment on, my Christian experience was to become a joy and a blessing. A joy seeing my prayers answered before my eyes by the mighty power of the Spirit of God rebuking demon spirits from oppressing the minds of poor mortals; and my becoming a gift bearer, or a blessing to the sinner, the helpless, the undeserving, through intercessory prayer, making available to them the sweet peace of God's love.

I, there and then, dedicated my life to being a peacemaker. "Blessed are the peacemakers," Jesus said, "for they shall be called the children of God" (Matthew 5:9). Heavenly peace is indeed a gift of great value, and lacking exceedingly in the lives of modern mortals. Our Lord Jesus placed great emphasis on the value of peace, as relating to the well-being of humans. Just before His crucifixion, He said to His disciples, "Peace I leave with you, my peace I give unto you" (John 14:27). And after His resurrection, His very first words to them in the upper room were, "Peace be unto you" (Luke 24:36). The apostle Paul declared the gospel of the Lord Jesus to be a gospel of peace (Romans 10:15). Above all, Christ Jesus is proclaimed as being "our peace" (Ephesians 2:14).

So, Christian friends, I ask you to make your presence felt wherever you find yourselves. Be a bearer of the gift of peace, to fellow mortals in this demon-agitated and trouble-filled world. Place those with whom you come in contact with under a heavenly atmosphere of light and peace. Demon spirits can't abide there, and as a result, the individuals will find peace and rest for their souls. Bring those that labor and are heavy laden to where Christ Jesus will give them rest.

Here is a short illustration. Business pressures were found to be demon-imposed pressures. Working on a telephone directory for about a month, I was not really concerned when told by the manager of a large building supply firm that it would be difficult for me to get to talk to the owner; I had a lot of time to work with and figured that if I came in two or three times a week, I would find the man free to talk over his advertising program one of those days.

Things didn't work out the way I had planned, and as I talked to the manager on Monday of that last week, I realized that I was facing an unusual situation. The boss was in, but was in a bad mood; too many things to attend to. The manager suggested that I call again the next day. I, in turn, asked for him to get me a definite appointment to see the man, or he could be left without advertising in the telephone directory for the coming year. He managed to get me a definite time—10:00 A.M., Wednesday morning.

Returning to keep my appointment that morning, I found myself arriving fifteen minutes early. It was a beautiful day, and up to then all had gone well. Entering the establishment, I found it to be a beehive of activity. Seeing the manager from a distance, I made my way to the counter where he was serving a customer. When a few feet away, he said good morning and I returned the salutation. He then asked a clerk to finish serving his customer, and we proceeded to walk up to the owner's office. His first words were that I was most unfortunate in coming to see the boss that day; it seemed that on the days I had come to see the man, something very upsetting had taken place and distressed him. "This morning," he said, "Joe must have gotten up on the wrong side of the bed, as he came in with a somber-looking countenance. A short while later, he got word that a shipment we had been expecting to receive today was delayed because of unexpected circumstances. So, if the boss shouts at you, don't pay attention to him; his distresses are probably the price he has to pay for being wealthy."

Arriving at the glassed-in office, the manager opened the door and told the owner, "The Yellow Pages man is here to keep the appointment I arranged with you last Monday."

"Come on in, but you'll have to wait until I get a phone call completed that I have to make right now. I don't know why but some of you guys pick the worst time to call on me."

"No problem, sir. I can wait, take your time," was my reply.

Sitting down, I realized that the man was operating on high voltage. He appeared to be a chain-smoker, as his office was filled with cigarette smoke, the ashtray overflowing with cigarette butts, and he had a cigarette in his hand. The tone of his phone conversation was loaded with outbursts of dissatisfaction toward the person he was talking to.

On a wall was a plaque with an interesting and appropriate little saying, which I cannot recall exactly; it made reference to the fact that the boss was soon to have a nervous breakdown—having worked at it, he was deserving of it. While that little statement was intended to be amusing, I took it as factual and accurate, and began working on my ministry of reconciliation as time permitted.

I projected the thoughts of my heart through the galaxies to the center of the universe to God, to that great planet where is located that heavenly temple, the abiding place of the King of kings, and began to converse with Christ Jesus in that Holy of Holies filled with the glory of the eternal throne. My conversation went something like this:

Precious Jesus, I need You, and I see this morning where You need me. I realize that You wish to bless the life of this precious rich man, but demon spirits have succeeded in having him all to themselves. You are following the rules of the game of life played between the forces of good and evil for the control of the minds of people, and in this particular case it places You where You are unable to shower this man's life with the sweet peace of Thy love. I thank the Lord that You have called me to be a bearer of Thy peace to fellow mortals living in this trouble-filled world, through the agency of prayer. Now Lord, by the merits of Thy precious blood shed on Calvary for the remission of sin, please forgive the iniquities and sins of this man sitting in my presence; and by the mighty power of the Holy Spirit, rebuke the demon spirits that are torturing his mind, and bless him with the sweet peace of Thy love. I thank Thee Lord for Thy blessings to us.

It wasn't more than five seconds that the man's conversation took on a new sense of direction. Instead of talking almost continually and shouting out unpleasantness, the tone of his voice abated to a sensible range, and he began to talk with what appeared to be intelligent reasoning, giving a chance to the party on the other end of the line to bring forth an explanation of his accomplishments, as I was soon to find out. The conversation closed on what appeared to be a tensionless note, and he hung up the phone.

"I am Dennis ________," he said as he stood up behind his desk, extending his hand toward me in a friendly way.

"Roger Morneau here," I said as I shook his hand with firmness.

"Nice meeting you, Roger, it's too bad you happen to come on a day when everything is running rough."

Really—I was amazed to see the change that had taken place in his personality. His stern-looking countenance that first appeared as some of those seen on monuments in city parks, had been replaced by one expressing a truly relaxed state of mind. A smile took form as he continued.

"I shouldn't be telling you this, but I think it will do me some good if I talk about it. From the moment I got up this morning, things began to upset me. First, I had some disturbing words with my wife over the breakfast table. I can't figure out why she was up that early today; she never gets up until after I am gone to work. Arriving at this place of business, aggravations started building up. And to top it all off, I got to looking over the books that have to do with my other businesses, and seeing the poor results we attained for the last quarter, I became angry and blew my top in talking to one of my managers, as you have witnessed; he was lucky to be able to give me sound reasons, showing that actions beyond his control had taken place in producing those lousy results, or I would have fired him regardless of the fact that he has a sick wife and five kids."

Then taking a deep breath as he was relaxing, he sat back in his reclining chair, saying, "Right now I feel great, a short while ago I felt as if I was carrying the world on my back. From now on I refuse to let anything upset me." He chuckled a bit over what he had said, and then preceded in lighting another cigarette.

We went on conversing, my bringing forth a couple of statements that were thought provoking and that caused the individual to ask questions that in turn gave me the opportunity to proceed into the spiritual, pointing him to the One that can change, wonderfully change, the most hopeless discouraging outlook. His declining the opportunity from then on to converse any longer on the spiritual led into our covering his advertising program as related to the various phases of his business, then I left for another call.

Getting into my car, I drove away and lifted up my heart to God in thanksgiving for my having been instrumental in His blessing the life of that poor rich man (poor in heavenly love, joy, and peace), benefiting him with the sweet peace of God's love, something he probably had never experienced.

Humanly speaking, the man had everything that money could buy that should make a person happy. But demon spirits were making sure that he couldn't enjoy the fruits of his labor. When I left him, he was joyful and hopeful. The Lord Jesus had gotten the demon spirits off his back (the expression—a little crude, but true). Again, the storm of life had abated and a much-needed calm had taken place by the power of Him who centuries back, marvelously displayed His capacity to bring about that desired end, when He commanded the turbulent Sea of Galilee, "Peace, be still!" (Mark 4:39).

The experience just stated is but one of many I have had, because of the many people I find myself coming in contact with in my work. For quite some time, I have been referring to such incidents as that of casting *off* devils. We read a great deal in the Bible about our Lord Jesus and His disciples having cast out devils.

In these modern times while demon possession is still experienced by certain individuals, it is taking place on a limited scale. Modern, scientific demons are using a new approach in carrying on their work of oppression and control upon humans; they work from the outside in, perplexing, distressing their minds, and wrecking their lives. In this way, their presence and actions are not recognized for what they truly are.

A while back I made the statement that as Christians passing through the land of the enemy, you and I have capacities or rights that no one else can exercise; not even the angels of heaven. That capacity, that right, consists of the ability to secure divine help from the throne of grace that can deliver fellow humans from the power and control of demon spirits.

The apostle Paul in his Epistle to the Ephesians declares that we wrestle not against flesh and blood, but against principalities, against the rulers of the darkness of this world, against spiritual wickedness in high places. He counsels on the importance of the Christian putting on the whole armor of God, then adds, "Praying always with all prayer and supplication in the Spirit, and watching thereunto with all perseverance and supplication for all saints" (see Ephesians 6:11–18).

Again, that same apostle in his First Epistle to Timothy makes an appeal to prayer for those outside the family of God. "I exhort therefore, that, first of all, supplications, prayers, intercessions, and giving of thanks, be made for all men. . . . For this is good and acceptable in the sight of God our Saviour; who will have all men to be saved, and to come unto the knowledge of the truth" (1 Timothy 2:1, 3, 4).

While Satan, the fallen cherub, became the rightful owner of this planet and its contents, as he once declared to our Lord Jesus (Luke 4:5–7) and is to continue ruling it until the second coming of Christ, his satanic influence and control over the lives of poor mortals can be broken by our prayers to Christ Jesus.

On the other hand, as our Lord does free individuals from that satanic captivity, we must be mindful of the fact that our great Redeemer will not press them into service to Himself. Jesus does not and will not force people to serve Him. He respects His Father's great gift to those created in His own image, freedom of choice.

The Bible makes it perfectly clear that God desires from all His creatures a service of love—homage that springs from an intelligent appreciation of His righteous character. The Lord takes no pleasure in a forced allegiance; to all people He grants freedom of choice that they may render Him voluntary service.

Keeping in mind the dual points just considered, I'd like to suggest that through our prayers to the Lord we place the people we are praying for in a position or situation where they can make intelligent decisions regarding their well-being in this present life and for eternity. I'd like to illustrate by telling a short experience.

Relaxing on grass and enjoying the beat of rock: Doped up and happy

A few years back, I was in Union Springs, New York, enjoying the opening of the annual New York Conference of Seventh-day Adventists camp meeting. It was a beautiful Sabbath day, one that had begun by my being brought out of dreamland by the sweet notes of an old favorite hymn, softly played over the public address system, enriched by the sounds of a deep-toned organ.

Stepping out of our cabin, I was met by a series of good wishes for the day, as the usual good morning salutation came from all sides on the part of brothers and sisters in Christ who were quickly moving on to prepare for the many wonderful moments of inspiration they were to receive in attending the spiritual convocations that were to take place that day.

The morning Sabbath services proved to be what I had hoped they would be—a savor of life unto life. These were the type of services that help one raise his sights. The eleven o'clock service having ended, we made our way out of the great pavilion enjoying the experience of shaking hands with longtime friends and acquaintances, many of whom we hadn't seen since the previous year. We had the added pleasure of having our noon meal with friends that my wife had invited to join us in consuming some of that expertly prepared vegetarian food she is so accustomed to providing.

So it was what could be referred to as a perfect day, until I met a gentleman from the western New York area later on that afternoon. He gave me a saddening bit of information in his answering my inquiry as pertaining to the Christian experience of a certain young man whom I had held in high esteem in years past during our stay in that part of New York State.

"Jack," he said, "is no longer the sharp young Christian man you have known him to be. As a college-educated individual doing well in building himself a good future in this present world, he has lost the love he had for the Lord; as he became more and more involved in his daily occupation, his interests changed. The influence of some ungodly individuals he associated with in his work rubbed off on him to the point that it changed his lifestyle outside of the work circle. His leisure time became occupied with activities that not only separated him from God, but also from his wife. Whether he left her, or she left him, that I don't exactly know, but they are no longer living together. He has become what is often called a modern swinger; and is living it up to the highest degree possible."

That account was indeed heart saddening, and I was searching my mind for words that could express my disappointment, when the gentleman continued.

"An additional bit of information may interest you. A fellow, who was in school with Jack a few years back, has reported that Jack has stated to him that he has one thousand dollars' worth of marijuana, and other good stuff in his home; he finds his relaxation in grass and enjoys the beat of rock music. Five thousand dollars sunk in a hi-fi stereo set gives him the impression of being in the front row of a rock concert. He is doped up and happy."

I could hardly believe my ears over the news I had received. My friend expanded on what he had said, by adding, "Don't feel too bad about him, he knew better than to get himself involved in a life of sin; he was brought up by God-fearing parents, wonderful commandment-keeping people. Jack wanted that kind of life or he would have done something about getting away from it in the beginning. I think he's a hopeless case. I have given up praying for him; I spend my time praying for more worthy individuals."

Then to reinforce his decision, he added, "In talking to his mother not long ago, I got the impression that she has slackened her praying over him. She feels that if Jack has chosen that kind of a life, there's nothing she can do about it."

Hearing about that gentleman giving up on the fellow, expressing it as openly as he did, I felt sorrow and hurt for the young man and was prompted in saying, "In other words, you feel that Jack is going to hell in high gear."

"Exactly—you couldn't have said it in more appropriate words."

We parted a few minutes later, and instead of going to a meeting that was about to begin and which I had planned to attend, I went back to our cabin to reflect on that most disturbing account. Being alone, I knelt and raised my heart to my great High Priest, Christ Jesus, bringing before Him that sad state of affairs regarding that precious young man. I asked the Lord to bless my mind with the power of His love, leading me to engage in a prayer ministry of daily intercession for Jack that would place him in a position to make intelligent decisions for this life and for eternity.

My prayer ended, and I lay on my bed and reflected on the matter. In my mind, I could hear the man's words, "I think he is a hopeless case. I have given up praying for him." *What powerful negative words,* I thought. I would have felt like giving up praying for the fellow also, were it not that I knew by experience that Christ Jesus is a mighty Redeemer, and specializes in hopeless cases. I had been one of those unpromising individuals, and how greatly the Spirit of God had wrought in my life to bless and to deliver from the hand of the destroyer.

A few minutes elapsed, and I decided on what course of action I should take. "Yes, that's it," experimental religion was needed here; a new prayer approach to solving a bad sin problem. While the Lord Jesus would not force Jack to serve Him because people ask Him to save the man, yet He could by the mighty power of His Holy Spirit in answer to specific daily prayers, free the fellow from the constant suggestions of demon spirits to wrong doing, and surround him with an atmosphere of heavenly grace, one that would be conducive to his making decisions for the right.

I realized that I must avoid falling into the inclination of praying in generalities, something that usually takes place when people have been praying for someone a long time. I figured that it could take months, even years, before Jack would reach a decision that the pleasures of a life of sin aren't worth the high cost he has to pay for it. I would have to be fervent and diligent in prayer to get him the help he needed every day. Demon spirits would not give up trying to keep him under their control, I figured.

From that day on, I rose a bit earlier each morning in order to seek divine help for the young man. My intercession went something like this, "Dear Jesus, I thank Thee at this time for the way You have blessed my life in calling me to practice Your ministry of reconciliation for fellow mortals traveling through the land of the enemy. I come before Thee at this time seeking special help for my young friend Jack, whom demon spirits have succeeded in leading into a life of sin. First, I pray that You will forgive his sins through the merits of Thy precious blood shed on Calvary for the remission of sin, until he finds himself in a position to ask for himself.

"Precious Jesus, by the mighty power of the Spirit of God, rebuke the demon spirits that are determined to control his life today, and surround the man with an atmosphere of heavenly grace. While Jack has no interest in God, and is giving himself up to enjoy the pleasures of sin, please send angels that excel greatly in power to those of Satan to protect him so he will not be destroyed.

"Bless the fellow's mind, Lord, so that wherein he has found his joy and relaxation in smoking grass and enjoying rock music, which has a satanic function, giving it power to fascinate, he may escape that satanic captivity. Heal that mind from the deterioration caused by the power of sin and the partaking of mind-altering substances, and elevate it to a level of capacity that will render it able to appreciate the sacred, the beautiful, and the divine to the degree that will be experienced by the redeemed from the earth through the ceaseless ages of eternity.

"Lord Jesus, whenever Jack finds himself assailed by demon spirits, I would appreciate very much if You would cause me to think of him sensing the urgency of the moment, so I can pray for him. Also Lord, bless the life of his dear wife according to her needs, and save them both into Thine eternal kingdom.

"Again, thank You for Your blessing in the lives of the people I pray for, and in causing me to see my prayers answered before my eyes. Amen."

Time has a way of changing days into weeks, and weeks into months, and months into years. Intercessory prayer through the merits of the precious blood of the Lord of glory shed on Calvary has the capacity to work miracles, overruling the forces of evil and affecting the miracle of redemption. So it was that two years from the time I had begun to pray for Jack and his wife, to my great amazement, as I was sitting in the great pavilion of the first Sabbath of camp meeting, I saw that precious couple walking hand in hand making their way in the direction of the pavilion to attend the morning service.

My heart leaped within me in a burst of joy as I saw them and became aware that I was seeing my prayers answered before my eyes. On that memorable day, I had the added joy of conversing with the young couple concerning the goodness of the Lord, but it was sometime later that I had the thrilling experience of hearing from Jack how the Spirit of God had operated in his life and worked in his behalf during the days of his forgetfulness of God.

"It was about two years ago," he said, "when I began to experience a change in the way I reasoned regarding my friends, my leisure time, my musical preferences, and other factors affecting my daily life.

"Up to then, for about four years, I had turned my mind from spiritual matters and given myself up to enjoying what is known by the world as the good life; or in other words, I was enjoying the pleasures of sin. And there was a superabundance of pleasures thrilling my life continually. From the moment I awoke each morning to the time I retired at night, I was involved in some form of self-gratification, or living in the anticipation of partaking in it. For instance, the very first thing I did after awaking was to turn on my hi-fi stereo set and play some of my favorite rock music, as I proceeded in getting ready for work; I felt it was groovy, and the beat of it satisfied an inner craving for that tempo. Every weekend was taken up with a wild party somewhere, roaring with women, liquor, grass, and whatever else could liven it up.

"By then my wife and I had broken up, and I was completely free to live my life the way I felt I could get the most enjoyment out of it. But about two years ago, things began to change. First, my rock music went flat on me. One evening, arriving home, I turned on my hi-fi, placed one of my favorite records on the turntable, and then sat comfortably with a glass of my favorite beverage in one hand and a newspaper in the other.

"I took a couple of sips from the glass, read a couple of minutes, and then sensed that something wasn't right—the music was not quite the same, something was missing. It wasn't enjoyable as it had been, so I checked the controls on the set. All was right, but my rock music had lost some of its appeal; yet I couldn't zero in on that missing element.

"The doorbell rang, and there was Albert, a close buddy, a self-pronounced rock music expert. I opened up, 'Albert, you came to visit at the right time. Something has gone wrong with my hi-fi set; it's not reproducing the music on this record in its entirety; it's missing something. I have probably played this record a thousand times, and I know there is something lacking from it this evening.'

"We played the record again, and halfway through it Albert began to laugh, then said, 'Jack, the time has come for you to sell me that stereo set. It's not performing to your liking anymore, but to me it's super. I have come to borrow one of your tools, I'll bring it back in a couple of days.'

"Having received the device, he left. I continued listening to additional rock records, realizing that they lacked that captivating essence they used to possess. The situation grew worse (or better depending on how one looks at it), and it came to the point that in a few months I actually hated rock music. In fact, one evening I dusted off the jackets of some of my old symphony records and from then on played them for relaxation."

Jack and I conversed together, and without my trying to get information out of him concerning his return to God, he continued filling me in on some details that in reality turned out to be direct answers to what I had asked the Lord to benefit his life with.

"Talk about God taking care of the undeserving," said Jack, "it's just plain amazing. I recall one particular instance when I lost control of my car when I passed through a pothole going down a hill; I thought it was the end of me. The car began zigzagging from one side of the road to the other, then headed directly for the abutment of a bridge railing, and veered off just in time to miss it by a few inches. An angel of the Lord must have taken charge of things, for I had no control of the car on the wet pavement."

After hearing his account of deliverance from destruction, I stated that the prayers of many of God's people must have been working in his behalf. Jack agreed, and then volunteered some additional information that led me to understand why a few times I woke up at night deeply impressed with a sense of urgency in praying for him; it happened that all of those instances were on Saturday nights, his partying time.

He continued his account, "At that time I had given up on God and eternal life, and had decided that having only this present life before me, I was going to enjoy it to the fullest, even if it meant killing myself in doing so. As I said before, every weekend I attended a wild party where anything went. I recall that one time when I was pretty well loaded with booze, the whole gang of us almost raising the roof with our music, singing, and all else, at about 1:00 A.M., something really strange happened to me. A couple of the gals were passing around a mixture of a beverage they claimed would thrill a person from one's toenails to the roots of his hair. When I was about to take the potion, a voice came from behind me, saying, 'Jack, don't you take that—if you do, it will kill you.' I felt a touch on my right shoulder as the words were spoken. I quickly turned around, and no one was there. That touch I felt on my shoulder sent a shiver through my whole body, and to my amazement, I instantly became as sober as if I hadn't taken a single drink. Feeling greatly out of place, I excused myself and left. As I was driving down the road, I realized that I didn't have the smell of liquor on my breath.

"That experience served to get me thinking. First, I realized that while I had given up on God, He hadn't given up on me. This was the beginning of my doing a lot of deep thinking regarding this present life versus eternity. The time came when I decided to talk the whole matter over with Lord Jesus, and to follow His leading. I had a lot of backtracking to do in order to get on the right road again. There was the matter of making things right with my wife and winning her back to me. It would take time to heal the old wounds and reestablish her confidence in me, but I figured it was worth the effort and that God would surely bless her life as He had blessed mine. I wouldn't be working alone.

"This day, I thank God for His love to us—being together is a reality."

Having heard the experience of Jack's returning to serving God, it brought great joy to my heart. It intensified my determination to carry on my prayer ministry of reconciliation, placing people where demon spirits couldn't control their lives. And besides, what joy it brought to my heart to see people blessed with the sweet peace of God's love. And I get a great deal of satisfaction from knowing that powerful demon spirits are rebuked and lose their hold on people because an ordinary mortal, little me, has conversed with the Ruler of the galaxies.

Prayer better than a super horn

Long-distance driving was beginning to get to me, especially when returning home on Friday afternoons after having been away from my family all week. One particular condition was in reality very frustrating, and would actually wear me out; I would get home very tired. This took place when traveling superhighways and I found myself unable to pass because of slow-moving traffic, and someone would actually block the passing lane making it impossible to keep up to the legal speed limit, which makes a big difference to a person having to travel five hours to get home.

The fact that people with large camping trailers or hauling boats behind their cars went five to eight miles per hour below the speed limit would not upset me; in fact, I admired their prudence in doing so. And I have found those people very considerate of others by keeping to the driving lane. But when an individual with a regular car would drive at the same speed in the passing lane, holding back a dozen cars or so from passing, it frustrated me greatly.

Then one day I was made aware of the existence of super horns; the type that could outdo air horns found on trucks. Humanly speaking, my problem was solved. I had a set installed under the hood of my new Subaru automobile and quickly discovered that I shouldn't use it near villages because it drove dogs almost crazy. At the sound of it, they would jump wildly and take off, knocking down youngsters and anything else in their way. It also had a good feature in that it was also useful in avoiding collisions with deer while traveling at night; the sound of the horn would cause them to clear the road in a great hurry.

Superhighway driving became a pleasure for me because I could always count on traveling at the speed limit. Then one day I had an experience that got me thinking.

On a Friday at about four o'clock in the afternoon, I was traveling north on Interstate 87, a few miles south of Albany, New York, when I came on a line of cars traveling the passing lane seven miles below the speed limit. The driving lane was loaded with big trucks, campers, passenger cars, motor homes, and so on. I followed my usual procedure in asking for passage; I turned on my left signal, and as I approached the last car, the driver pulled into the driving lane, giving me the chance of accomplishing what he had hoped for, getting ahead.

The same procedure was followed for about twenty additional vehicles, and then I came up to the number one car, a black Cadillac occupied by four women probably in their fifties. The driver behaved as if she was the only one on the road and was in no particular hurry to get anywhere, and seemed to enjoy the experience of relaxing in the passing lane.

After four or five minutes, I turned on my headlights, keeping the left signal going. A couple of minutes later, I blew my regular car horn to see if I could get the woman's attention. She looked in her rearview mirror then flipped the night vision feature on, and continued at the same rate of speed.

To my right, in the driving lane, was a station wagon carrying a couple and two youngsters of about ten and twelve years of age. The little folks were having a great time watching me try to get Mrs. Cadillac to let me pass. A few minutes went by, then I decided to use the super horn to ask for passage. I pressed on the button and held it there a moment. The woman was greatly startled and undoubtedly pressed the accelerator to the floor, as the car actually shot ahead, zigzagged, and I thought for a moment it was going to roll over. But the driver managed to hold it on to the shoulder of the road and pavement, and then having regained her composure, pulled off the road and let the traffic go by.

I had obtained passage, but I felt terrible at the thought that I had almost caused an accident that could have cost the women their lives. During the remainder of the way, I couldn't think about anything else. As my custom was, and still is, I conversed in prayer with my great High Priest, Christ Jesus, thanking Him for His angels having kept the black Cadillac from turning over. Then I said, "Precious Jesus, there has to be a better way for me to clear a passing lane than using that super horn. I can't take the chance of causing an accident. If there is a better way of reaching my objective, please bless my mind that I may be made aware of it. I thank You for blessing my life in so many ways. Amen."

As I was reflecting on the matter, it wasn't long before I came to understand where the root of the problem lay. Demon spirits have great advantage over people who do not govern their lives by following God's great principles of love. So, if demon spirits can aggravate them to the point that they have a hard time living with themselves, then getting on a superhighway the same spirits make them feel like driving in the passing lane reasoning that they have the right to do so, seeing they pay taxes and the road is theirs; then the possibility of an accident taking place is very great. I recalled an instance where I saw a couple of small cars driving on the shoulder of the road to pass such a person.

I came to the conclusion that prayer was the right answer to my problem—not a super horn. And time has proven my decision to have been correct. Now when I come upon a congested passing lane, I see it as a call to prayer, and refer to the experience as my entering a prayer zone. Immediately, I project my thoughts to that heavenly temple and begin to converse with Christ Jesus, my great High Priest. My appeal regarding help for the needy usually goes this way, "Dear Jesus, it is such a privilege for me to come before Thy divine majesty having no interrupted access to Your wealth of divine grace for the descendants of Adam who are perplexed and distressed by demon spirits, and are carrying a heavy burden of sin. Up ahead of this line of cars is a precious individual just about worn out by the constant inspiration of demon spirits, who are determined to even up one's life of misery by being a distress in the lives of others. So, that driver's revenge is carried out by holding back people who are in need of reaching their destination on time.

Jesus, please forgive that individual's iniquities and remove his or her burden of sin, rebuke the demon spirits who have been making sport of that person, and shower him or her with the sweet peace of Thy love. I thank Thee, Lord, for having called me to pray for that needy individual, and also for You always blessing people beyond what I have the ability to ask. Amen."

I never ask the Lord to have the individual move into the driving lane so I can pass. I have come to realize that as long as a person is determined to sow distress in the lives of others, that person is having a bad struggle with demon spirits; they resist giving up their control over them. Therefore, I continue praying, asking the Lord to bless that individual with an abundance of heavenly grace, and by the mighty power of His Holy Spirit, to break the power struggle put forth by the spirits to maintain their hold on their victim.

In most cases, I haven't had the time to cover the first part of my request for the individual before they have moved into the driving lane. I get great satisfaction from knowing that my prayer to the Lord Jesus has put to flight demon spirits that have been sowing distress in the lives of poor mortals for centuries.

Repairing a torn heart without surgery

Seeing Thomas, a Christian friend of many years, at camp meeting time was always an experience I looked forward to from year to year. Many years back, we had attended the same church and spent much time together.

His life was ruled by sound Christian principles I admired, and above all, his consideration for others was remarkable; in all the years I had known him, not once had I heard him raise his voice in dissatisfaction or unkindness toward anyone. Once I asked him how he managed to keep his cool under conditions that would be likely to upset most anyone, and why he appeared so choosy in his use of words.

"Roger," he said, "I believe the Good Book, which says, 'If any man offends not in word, the same is a perfect man' [James 3:2]. I understand this to mean perfection in the field of human relations, and that's quite a goal to work toward; getting along with people is always on my mind."

His statement made a lasting impression on me. This one year as I met Tom on the camp grounds, I found him to have lost his usually lively countenance, and he seemed to be carrying a heavy load of care.

"Tom, how have you been since I last saw you?"

"OK, I guess."

"Are you feeling well? Where is that continuous smile you used to have?"

"Roger, I would like to talk to you sometime about a problem I have."

"Let's not lose any time, what do you say we go for a walk?"

"That's fine with me."

We proceeded away from the congested area to where we could converse without being interrupted.

"Roger, I am scared to death—I am afraid that my marriage of thirty years is going to break up."

"Because of what?" I said. Without answering my question, he continued.

"If my wife leaves, it will destroy me, and bring great unhappiness in the lives of our children. My heart is half torn out of me now."

By then I was getting weak in the legs, and started to look for a place to sit down; I was shocked.

He continued, "It's hard to believe, but my wife misunderstands most everything I say to her. For instance, a couple of weeks back, I had in mind to take her out for dinner on the weekend; but I couldn't recall if she had to work that Sunday or not because her schedule keeps changing. So I asked her about it. She got angry at me, saying that I get pleasure from her having to work. Then she burst out of the room without my having a chance to ask her if she would like to eat out. I can't figure it out, but somehow she reads words into what I say that aren't really there. In addition to all that, a statement she made last week brought the roof down on me; she mentioned that she can hardly stand the tone of my voice anymore, she finds it so irritating."

I realized as Tom was telling me of his difficulties that indeed he had a serious problem facing him.

"Roger," he continued, "do you think that my voice has changed in the last year?"

"Tom, your voice has not changed as far as I can tell, but it may have for your wife. Do you know of anything else that may be distressing her? Is she having difficulties at work that you know of?"

"Her work has always been more or less a touchy subject. She often talks about one woman in particular that is a constant troublemaker, and what gets to my wife is that the woman is a church officer in one of the prominent churches in the community."

"That may be where much of her difficulties originate, and you get the overspill at home. Does any other person notice your wife's distress besides you?"

"Yes, a few weeks back we had some friends over, and I felt bad for the woman when after her having made a statement, my wife misunderstood her and went on to straighten her out, though the woman insisted that she didn't mean it the way my wife had taken it. That made me feel awful, because the folks have been friends of ours for a long time. After leaving our place, my wife gave a wrong application to most everything our friends had talked about."

"I agree with you, Tom, you have a serious problem in your home. I think that your wife needs help from a qualified person who is knowledgeable in dealing with such difficulties. This is the best advice I can give you. And the sooner you take that step, the better off you both will be."

"I agree with you to a certain point. Let me tell you of an experience that took place last week. All day long I had been thinking over this matter while working. Arriving home, I cleaned up and then had a word of prayer with the Lord on how I should go about getting my wife to agree to see a doctor, counselor, minister, or any professional who could help us. Then sitting in my rocker, I tried reading the evening newspaper, but my mind kept reverting back to our problem. Then I was carried back twenty years ago, to the time when you and I and Joe ______ were doing some painting in the church. As we were painting away, you and Joe had a conversation about how people's thoughts are not always one's own creation. You made a statement that the way people think and the way they feel is highly influenced by the actions of supernatural beings. Your statement stayed with me a long time, but eventually I forgot about it, and it seemed that it coming back to me last week is an indication of the Lord that you may have the key to unlocking the door to the source of our difficulties. I know that the Lord has blessed your life in converting you from spiritism, and because of your past dealings with evil spirits, your guidance may be just what we need. I have a question for you. Do you think that fallen angels could be the cause of my wife reasoning and misunderstanding people the way she does?"

As Tom was speaking, I sent a quick SOS to Lord Jesus, *Please bless and guide my mind, O Lord, my Strength and my Redeemer.* Instantly, I thought of a way to proceed.

"Tom, I believe that Lord Jesus has help ready for you. Your wife is a fine Christian person and loves the Lord. During your days at camp meeting, you both will receive great inspiration, and as you are encouraged in the Lord, I would like you to watch for an opportunity to make an appeal to your wife for carrying on a prayer ministry for the spiritual well-being of that woman at work who is a great source of irritation to her. [I explained the ministry further to him.] To answer the question you have asked a few moments ago, my answer is Yes. Fallen angels can cause people to misunderstand others.

"Let's take a minute and consider two motivating factors about demon spirits and their activities. First, they find pleasure in bringing misery and destruction in the lives of mortals. Second, demon spirits find great delight in stirring up human emotions to heights sufficient to create anger or hatred capable of murder (according to a satanic priest).

"Now, I believe that you will agree with me that if demon spirits are able to work on human minds in a way to produce anger or hatred capable of murder, they should have no difficulties in causing individuals to misunderstand others."

"That sounds logical, tell me more."

"Let's consider the woman at work who is a source of irritation to your wife, and how she is being used to do the demon spirits' work. There are two great human weaknesses that can be open avenues for the spirits to use individuals to carry out their work of misery and mind oppression in humans.

"First, some people rule their lives by listening to their feelings. If they feel like telling someone off, they go and do it.

"Second, certain individuals speak out everything (thoughts) that enter their minds, and sow distress in the lives of others, wounding and destroying. An unsanctified tongue is spoken of in the Word of God as being as destructive as fire, and as deadly as poison" (see James 3:5, 8).

"Roger, what you are saying makes a lot of sense, but I find it hard to believe that a Christian woman, who prays to the Lord every day, could be influenced by demons to do their work."

"Tom, I am inclined to feel the way you do here, but when I think that one of our Lord's apostles was controlled by a demon while he walked with Jesus for more than three years [John 6:70] and became demon possessed during the Last Supper, as the Bible says, 'Satan entered into him' [John 13:27], then I became very concerned over the influence demon spirits can have over fervent church-attending people."

"Now I agree with you completely. What do you suggest that I do?"

"I suggest that you begin by taking this matter to the Lord Jesus in prayer, asking for the power of His Holy Spirit to bless both your minds with the sweet peace of His love. For yourself, ask to be blessed with tact—that delicate perception of the right thing to say or do without offending. You will need that capacity in order to convince your wife that she should engage in a prayer ministry for the woman she works with. From then on, one of the first things you need to do each morning is to ask the Lord Jesus to bless both of you by the power of His Spirit with the heavenly graces that adorn His character; consisting of heavenly love, heavenly joy, heavenly peace, long-suffering, gentleness, goodness, faith, meekness, and temperance, which is in the fullest sense of the word, self-control—consisting of the ability to check and regulate, to restrain and govern self in all aspects of life. As your minds are being blessed daily by the mighty power of the Spirit of God, demon spirits will lose their power to upset and distress."

"Roger, you are giving me such hope in seeing my problem solved by the power of God, I'm getting all excited about it."

"Tom, I believe you will see great changes taking place in your home."

One week went by, and on the following Sabbath as I met Tom, he was all smiles again and the very first words he said to me were, "It's working, it's working!"

I am happy to say that almost a decade has passed since that incident took place in Tom's life, and by the grace of God, it's still working. Tom has regained his continuous smile, and both he and his wife are reflecting the heavenly graces that adorn the character of the Lord Jesus in their daily lives.

Carrying on a prayer ministry for fellow sojourners traveling through the land of the enemy, how rewarding it is.

"How beautiful upon the mountains are the feet of him that bringeth good tidings, that publisheth peace; that bringeth good tidings of good, that publisheth salvation; that saith unto Zion, Thy God reigneth!" (Isaiah 52:7).

La Fin

Appendix

Brief Bible Readings for Busy People—No. 2

THE PROPHECY OF DANIEL TWO

1. May we understand prophecy? 2 Peter 1:19, 20.
2. What did Christ say of Daniel's prophecy? Matt. 24:15.
3. Why was Nebuchadnezzar troubled? Dan. 2:1. (Read verses 1-35.)
4. Who gave this dream to the king? Dan. 2:28.
5. What was the dream to reveal? Dan. 2:29.
6. Whom did the head of gold represent? Dan. 2: 37, 38. Note 1.
7. What kingdoms were to follow Babylon? Dan. 2:39, 40. Note 2.
8. What did the silver (breast and arms) represent? Dan. 5:28-31.
9. How long did Medo-Persia rule? From 538-331 B.C.
10. What did the brass symbolize? Grecia. (See Dan. 8:20, 21.)
11. What empire followed Grecia? Rome. D 8:23-25; Luke 2:1-4. Note 3.
12. What change was to come to the kingdom Dan. 2:41, 42. Note 4.
13. How would these kings try to strength selves? By intermarriage. Dan. 2:43
14. What eternal kingdom was to be set u days of these kings? Dan. 2:44.
15. What represented this eternal kingdom dream? Dan. 2:45.
16. What must take place before Christ's ki established? Matt. 24:14.

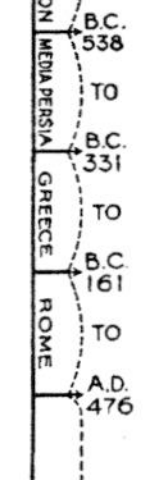

TEN KINGDOMS OF EUROPE

2nd COMING OF CHRIST

Notes on Reading No. 2

Note 1 (Dan. 2:37, 38).—Jer. 27:1-11, God gave the kingdom to Nebuchadnezzar. Eze. 26:7-11, the fall of Tyre. Eze. 29:18, 19, Egypt given as wages for work against Tyre.

Note 2 (Dan. 2:39).—Jer. 51:11, 27, 28, downfall of Babylon foretold and Medes named. Isa. 45:1-3, Cyrus named 113 years before he was born. Jer. 51:45, 46, God's sign to His children. Isa. 47: 5-13, the doom of the city. Dan. 5:1-28, the night of pleasure. Jer. 51:14, the entry of the army. Jer. 51:31, 32, the announcement taken to the king. Jer. 51:30, the failure of the Babylonian army to defend the city. Jer. 50:35, 37, 46; 51:53-58; Isa. 13:17-22, the destruction of Babylon.

Note 3.—The historian Gibbon says: "The arms of the republic, sometimes vanquished in battle, always victorious in war, advanced with rapid steps to the Euphrates, the Danube, the Rhine, and the Ocean; and the images of gold, or silver, or brass, that might serve to represent the nations and their kings, were successively broken by the iron monarchy of Rome."—Edward Gibbon, *Decline and Fall*, vol. 3, p. 161.

Note 4.—The following took possession of the territory of Western Rome: A.D. 351, Franks, France; Alemanni, Germany; A.D. 406, Burgundians, Switzerland; Suevi, Portugal; Vandals in northern part of Africa; A.D. 408, Visigoths, Spain; A.D. 449, Anglo-Saxons, England; A.D. 483, Ostrogoths, Italy; Lombards, part of Italy; Heruli, part of Italy.

Cyril and Cynthia kept the actual Bible study guide they used in 1946, *Brief Bible Readings for Busy People.* This is no. 2.

Brief Bible Readings for Busy People

The Order of Bible Studies Given

1. The Word of God (2 Timothy 3:16, 17)
2. Daniel 2 (2 Peter 1:19, 20)
3. The Second Coming (Hebrews 9:28)
4. Signs of Christ's Coming (Matthew 24:3)
5. The Millennium (1 Thessalonians 4:15–17)
6. Destiny of the Wicked* (Romans 6:23)
7. Home of the Saved* (Matthew 5:5)
8. Daniel 7 and the Little Horn* (Daniel 7:1–7)
9. Christ, Our High Priest (Hebrews 8:13)
10. The Investigative Judgment (Matthew 16:27)
11. The Law and the Gospel* (Psalm 103:19)
12. The Sabbath (Genesis 2:1–3)
13. Sabbath and the New Testament (John 15:10)
14. Origin of Sunday Observance (Isaiah 14:14)
15. Origin of Evil Angels (Ephesians 2:2)
16. Good Angels; Their Work (Revelation 5:11)
17. The Nature of Man, State of the Dead (Genesis 2:2)
18. Spiritualism (Hebrews 1:7)
19. Controversy Between Christ and Satan* (Revelation 12:1)
20. Seal of God, Mark of the Beast (2 Timothy 2:19)
21. The Christian's Duty (John 1:12)
22. Jesus Saves the Lost (Romans 6:23)
23. Faith (Hebrews 11:1)
24. Ordinances of the Church (Matthew 28:19)
25. Precious Promises* (Titus 1:2)
26. The Body Temple (Exodus 25:8)
27. Acceptable Prayer (Psalm 62:8)
28. Work of the Holy Spirit (John 15:26)

* Study or page was missing.

Topics found in the Bible study guide used—*Brief Bible Readings for Busy People.*

When Roger Arrived, He Was Delighted Over His Experience With The Spirits. He Showed Us That Beautiful Writing On The Paper, And Said," I Am Going To Frame This Piece Of Paper; I Have Never Seen Such Beautiful Freehand Writing In My Life."

Then Turning To The Priest He Asked This Question: "I Wonder Why The Spirit Didn't Give Me The Phone Number As Well As The Location Address?"

The Satanic Priest Spoke Up Saying, "You Did Not Ask The Spirit For It. According To Thy Faith Be It Done Unto Thee." He Then Continued In These Words; "The Experience You Have Had This Evening Is Child Play, In Comparison To What The Gods Have In Mind For You Two Gentlemen. But You Have To Exercise Faith In The Spirits And Expect Great Things From Them. What Is Needed In Your Life Is To Witness The Spirits' Power And Intelligence At Work A Few Times, Then I Believe You Will Be Able To Exercise A Sufficient Amount Of Faith So They Will Work For You In Great Ways."

Roger wrote this whole book by hand. Here is a page from the manuscript (the name of his friend "Roger" was changed to "Roland").

One of the merchant ships Roger worked on—the *Walter B. Reynolds.*

LIST OR MANIFEST OF ALIENS EMPLOYED ON THE VESSEL AS MEMBERS OF CREW

W.B. Reynolds

A United States Immigrations document listing alien employees. The vessel—*W.B. Reynolds*—arrived in Oswego, New York, from Montreal on April 23, 1945. This is the same ship he worked on prior to being drafted. Roger's name is listed near the bottom, showing length of service at sea (3 months), position (fireman), age (19), race (French), nationality (Canada), height, and weight. Several other ship manifest documents on file include his name up until November 1945.

AWARDS—CANADIAN ARMY (ACTIVE) M

500M—1-44 (3467) H.Q. 1772-45-8

SURNAME (IN BLOCK LETTERS)	CHRISTIAN NAMES	REG. NO.	RANK ON DISCHARGE	FILE NO. C.A.S.F. UNIT
MORNEAU, 19 - 5'10 - Bruns- Noirs	Roger	C.124885	Pte.	40-91930

WAR SERVICE BADGE (CLASS) ELIGIBLE G.S.C. NO. 182715 DATE DESPATCHED: Issued at D.D.4 1-2-45

ADDRESS:

CAMPAIGN MEDALS	REGISTRATION NUMBER AND DATE DESPATCHED
War Medal 1939-45	

(THE REVERSE TO BE USED FOR ESTATE PURPOSES)

Roger was given a medal for his service in the Canadian army, issued on February 1, 1945, at District Depot no. 4 (Montreal). This form shows his rank (Private) and age (19) at discharge.

M.F.M. 7 (FR)
25M—5-44 (4668)
H.Q. 1772-39-1653

ARMÉE CANADIENNE (ACTIVE)

CERTIFICAT DE LIBÉRATION

Les présentes certifient que Roger MORNEAU (nom en entier)

matricule C-124885 grade SOLDAT

s'est engagé(e) dans " ROYAL CANADIAN ARMY SERVICE CORPS "

L'ARMÉE CANADIENNE (ACTIVE), à Kingston Ont. le 22nd

jour de Juillet 19 44;

a servi au CANADA

et est maintenant libéré(e) du service en vertu de l'ordre de service courant N° 1029., Para. 5.

pour cause de " POUR REINTEGRER LA VIE CIVILE "
Pour remplir des fonctions d'importances Nationales"
AUTHY:A.&.Q.Camp Borden Letter CB. 40-M-5363 (SCA)d/10-12-44.

SIGNALEMENT à la DATE ci-après mentionnée:—

Age 19 Ans 9 Mois

Taille 5' 10"

Teint Medium

Yeux Bruns

Cheveux Noirs

Marques ou cicatrices

Tatouage aux bras

Roger Morneau
Signature du militaire

Date de la libération 1er Fevrier 1945

No. 4 District Depot, C.A. FEB 1 1945 Montreal, P.Q.

for (S. ECHENBERG), Colonel,
Officier qui délivre le certificat
COMMANDING No. 4 DISTRICT DEPOT, (CA).
Grade

Date 1er Fevrier 194 5

N.B.—Comme il n'est pas délivré de duplicata de ce certificat, quiconque trouve ce document est prié de le transmettre sous pli non affranchi au Bureau des Archives, ministère de la Défense Nationale, Ottawa, Canada.

DUPLICATA POUR DOSSIER

(T.S.V.P.)

Roger's discharge certificate from the Canadian army, showing his enlistment date (July 22, 1944—Kingston, Ontario), where he served (Canada), and the reason for his discharge: "To return to civil life—to engage in work of national importance." The certificate (dated February 1, 1945) indicates a letter from Camp Borden (dated December 10, 1944).

His final interview document (Department of Pensions and National Health, dated January 31, 1945) includes this statement: "Morneau is a slender, well built individual. He is a bilingual, 19 years old lad whose conversation indicates a good native ability and maturity beyond his years. Upon discharge he is returning to the Merchant Marine, about which he appears most enthusiastic. He is well-qualified at this type of work."